WARRIOR 173

MAMLUK 'ASKARI 1250–1517

DAVID NICOLLE   ILLUSTRATED BY PETER DENNIS

Series editor Marcus Cowper

First published in Great Britain in 2014 by Osprey Publishing,
PO Box 883, Oxford, OX1 9PL, UK
PO Box 3985, New York, NY 10185-3985, USA
E-mail: info@ospreypublishing.com

A CIP catalogue record for this book is available from the British Library.

ISBN: 978 1 78200 928 3
E-book ISBN: 978 1 78200 929 0

Editorial by Ilios Publishing Ltd, Oxford, UK (www.iliospublishing.com)
Index by Zoe Ross
Typeset in Myriad Pro and Sabon
Artwork by Peter Dennis
Originated by PDQ Media, UK
Printed in China through Worldprint Ltd

14 15 16 17 18 10 9 8 7 6 5 4 3 2 1

www.ospreypublishing.com

DEDICATION

Dr Shihab al-Sarraf, a true pioneer.

ARTIST'S NOTE

Readers may care to note that the original paintings from which the colour
plates in this book were prepared are available for private sale. The
Publishers retain all reproduction copyright whatsoever. All enquiries
should be addressed to:

Peter Dennis, Fieldhead, The Park, Mansfield, Notts, NG18 2AT
magie.h@ntlworld.com

The Publishers regret that they can enter into no correspondence upon this
matter.

EDITOR'S NOTE

With 'Mamluk and 'mamluk' the former has been used when referring to the
sultanate or the state or period in general. Whenever anything is specific to
only the *mamluk* warrior, the latter has been used.

CONTENTS

INTRODUCTION   4

CHRONOLOGY   11

RECRUITMENT   13

ORGANIZATION   21

BELIEF AND BELONGING   26

APPEARANCE AND EQUIPMENT   34

TRAINING AND CAMPAIGNING   40

EXPERIENCE OF BATTLE   50

COLLECTIONS AND SIGNIFICANT HISTORICAL LOCATIONS   56

FURTHER READING   58

GLOSSARY   62

INDEX   64

MAMLUK 'ASKARI
1250–1517

INTRODUCTION

Mamluks, or *ghulams* as they were also called, are generally described by Western writers as 'slave soldiers'. The rulers of the Mamluk Sultanate of Egypt and Syria, and the comparable Delhi Sultanate of northern India, are sometimes referred to as 'slave kings'. However, this description reflects a fundamental misunderstanding of the concept of 'slavery' in medieval Islamic civilization. Here it is worth noting that the Mamluk Sultanate did not call itself such. Instead, one of its official names was *Dawlat al-Turkiyya* – 'The State of the Turks' – which highlights the importance of their Turkish origins to the Mamluk ruling class, at least from the mid-13th to the mid-14th century.

Slavery or bonded labour played a minor part in agriculture in Islamic lands. However, those of slave origin played a significant role in domestic life, the service of the elite and, of course, in the military. Furthermore, it became

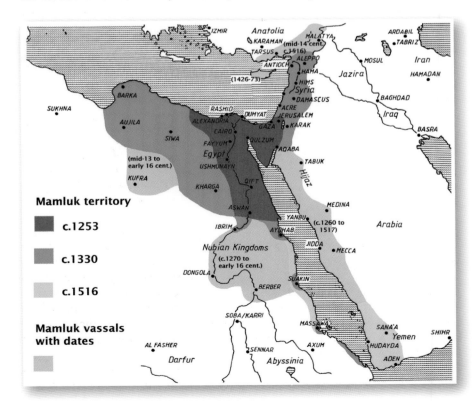

Mamluk territory

- c.1253
- c.1330
- c.1516

Mamluk vassals with dates

Bridge over the Abu'l-Managga irrigation canal between Cairo and Shubra, built during the reign of the al-Zahir Baybars al-Bunduqdari in 1266 and decorated with carved lions, a motif identified with Baybars. (Author's photograph)

commonplace for individuals who had once been legally slaves to rise to positions of influence and authority, though states ruled by such men remained rare. This phenomenon seems bizarre to a modern Western world but underpinning it was a form of slavery far removed from that seen in classical Greece, Rome and much of the Western world. Above all, the relationship between a slave, or freedman-client as he typically became, and his master-patron was very different in medieval Islamic societies.

Medieval Islamic slavery was not based upon the master's ownership of the slave's body and labour, but upon a concept of patronage which, although not between equals, nevertheless imposed obligations on both parties. In somewhat idealized medieval Islamic legal terms, both parties were *mawali* (sing. *mawla*), a superior *mawla* and an inferior *mawla*, and their relationship was supposedly a sort of alliance. This ethical concept enabled slaves to have legal rights, almost as if they had been adopted as 'foster sons' by a master who accepted legal obligations as their 'foster father'.

Study of the history and culture of the Mamluk Sultanate has suffered from Western scholars' deeply engrained abhorrence of perceived 'slave rule'. However, in reality, the medieval Islamic world had a distinctive basis of authority, especially in the Mamluk Sultanate where legitimacy of rule was a prize to be won, like any other. Rarely inherited by ties of blood, it could be confirmed by a ruler's behaviour and piety, and by the effectiveness of his government. What is even less understood today is the degree to which women of the Mamluk elite played significant cultural and even religious roles as patrons.

In much the same way, the loyalty of leaders and troops could not simply be inherited by the successor of a preceding ruler. It had to be earned, or at least purchased, as political and military loyalty was much more fluid than in medieval European societies – hence the Mamluks' largely undeserved reputation for disloyalty amongst many pre-modern European commentators. Loyalty was almost democratic, being based upon respect, obligation, fellow feeling and rewards. The Islamic chronicles also make clear that emotion played a major role as friendship was undoubtedly a major feature in group solidarity within *mamluk* society.

Scholars still wrestle with the question of whether the translation 'slave' – with all its associations for modern readers – is suitable for *mamluk* soldiers,

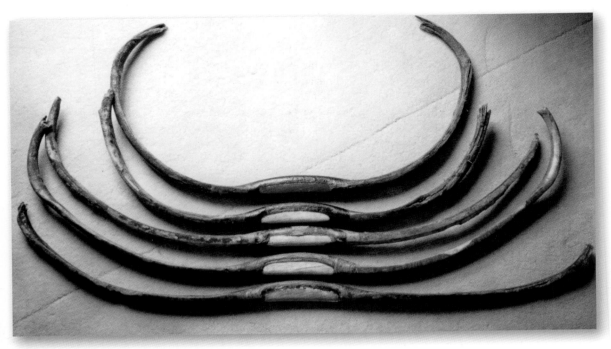

Mid-13th to early 14th-century composite bows from Qal'at al-Rahba. (Qatar Museums Authority, Doha; author's photographs)

even in the early years of their individual careers. In a *mamluk* context, the term 'slave' normally referred to an originally unfree status, not a current one. Furthermore, the word's most common associations were with obedience and faithfulness, characteristics that reflected a patrimonial rather than a feudal society.

In practical terms this meant that elite military units within the Mamluk army might better be described as households rather than regiments. The great medieval Arab historian Ibn Khaldun (1332–1406) echoed these positive attitudes when writing about *mamluks*:

> It was by the grace of Allah … that He came to the rescue of the True Faith, … restoring in Egypt the unity of the Muslims, guarding His order and defending His ramparts. This He did by sending to them, out of this Turkish people and out of its mighty and numerous tribes, guardian amirs and devoted defenders who are imported as slaves from the lands of heathendom to the lands of Islam… They embrace Islam with the determination of true believers, while retaining their nomadic virtues, which are undefiled by vile nature, unmixed with the filth of lustful pleasures, unmarred by the habits of civilization, with their youthful strength unshattered by excess of luxury.

Who, then, were these troops? Christian Europe was regarded as unsuitable as a source for large numbers of 'slave' recruits, and until the 14th century European recruits were commonly regarded as physically ugly, habitually disloyal and generally unreliable. Sub-Saharan Africa had previously been a source of recruits for Egypt and North Africa. However, these were used almost solely as infantry because, as yet, Africans had virtually no cavalry tradition. Non-Islamic India could also be a major source, but Indian *mamluks* or *ghulams* were rarely seen beyond the Islamic states of India itself, neighbouring Afghanistan and eastern Iran.

In contrast, the steppes of south-eastern Europe, and central and inner Asia offered a suitable and substantial pool of potential recruits. As Sa'id al-Andalusi wrote of the Turks during the first half of the 12th century: 'The Turks are also a nation having a large population (second only to the Chinese)… They distinguish themselves by their ability to wage war and by the construction of arms, and by being the ablest horsemen and tacticians.'

In the 10th century these Turks were well known to Muslim scholars such as al-Khwarazmi, who noted that the Turkic peoples of the western steppes had long been under Iranian cultural influence. In reality, this influence had been mutual, as there had been a prolonged Turkish influence upon at least the military aspects of Iranian civilization. At the same time, there may have been some differentiation between truly 'enslaved' recruits from more distant tribes who came via the Oghuz and Kipchaq states, and Oghuz or Kipchaq recruits who accepted the status of *mamluk* more willingly in the knowledge that it could open up glittering career prospects.

Kipchaqs had been widely employed as soldiers even before the Mongol conquest of the Kipchaq tribal states, having been seen in the Byzantine Empire, eastern Europe and the Islamic world. Following the Mongol catastrophe of the early 13th century, however, Kipchaq recruits were far more numerous and probably formed the bulk of those enlisted by the early Mamluk Sultanate. They came from an area known to Persian speakers as *Dasht-i Kipçak* (the Kipchaq Desert), steppe grasslands with a little agriculture and some urban centres. These steppes were crossed by several trade routes and the natives were thus in contact with a large part of the known world. Kipchaq culture, like that of the other Turkish-speaking steppe peoples, was characterized by a social system where patterns of loyalty and individual attachment were both personal and communal. These people were not territorial, and so it was relatively easy for a *mamluk* recruit to transfer his loyalties to a new person or community.

Although the *mamluk* phenomenon could be found across virtually the entire medieval Islamic world, the version that emerged in Egypt and produced the remarkably successful Mamluk Sultanate, might have had its primary origins in the Fatimid Caliphate. The Fatimids had ruled Egypt and dominated much of North Africa and Syria for several centuries before being overthrown in the late 12th century by Saladin, the founder of the Ayyubid dynasty. The Ayyubids

Maristan hospital of al-Qaymari in the suburb of Salihiya overlooking Damascus. It was sponsored by Sayf al-Din Yusuf al-Qaymari, the Kurdish *amir* who invited the Mamluk Sultan Qutuz into Damascus to face the Mongol invasion in 1260. (Author's photograph)

Pieces of wood, from the 13th to the mid-14th centuries, that were in the process of being shaped to form the cores of composite bows but never completed. These examples are from the Citadel of Damascus. (Syrian National Museum Conservation Department, Damascus; author's photograph)

took over and then refined the Fatimid military system, abandoning the recruitment of African *mamluk* infantry but greatly extending their recruitment of Turkish cavalry. Saladin's successors thereby established a *mamluk* army that then replaced the ailing Ayyubid Sultanate with its own Mamluk Sultanate.

To understand the Mamluk army one must first understand the fragmented Ayyubid armies from which it emerged. The term *'askar* could refer to the unit garrisoning, or paid, by a town, as it would have done for centuries, and these early *'askaris* would not normally be considered part of the military elite. The *'askar* of an Ayyubid ruler, however, consisted of professional, full-time *'askaris*. The most highly regarded of them were by this time largely of *mamluk* origin, though their numbers could still be remarkably small.

 THE BATTLE OF 'AYN JALUT (3 SEPTEMBER 1260)

The battle of 'Ayn Jalut was hard fought and far from being an inevitable Muslim victory. Both sides were relatively evenly matched, though the Mongols probably had superior numbers of cavalry while the Mamluk Sultanate fielded significant infantry forces. Several factors eventually tipped the balance, including the Mamluk commanders' better knowledge of the terrain – Baybars was especially knowledgeable as he had spent much time in exile in the area. The Mongol commander, Kitbuqa, also made a tactical error by pursuing an apparently retreating part of the Mamluk army and thus allowing his forces to become surrounded in difficult country. Once the Mamluk trap had been sprung, the remarkable discipline and cohesion of units of élite *'askaris* (**1** and **2**) under experienced *amirs* (**3**) meant that the surrounded Mongols (**4**) were unable to break through the *mamluk* lines. Under such circumstances, the well-equipped, well-trained and relatively heavily armoured *'askaris* held firm against increasingly desperate Mongol charges.

Ceramic fragments from the medieval potters' quarter in southern Cairo. At least 12 of these include Mamluk heraldic insignia. (Cinquantenaire Museum, Brussels; author's photograph)

Whereas the role of freeborn Kurdish troops in Ayyubid armies has often been exaggerated, it is clear that Turks were consistently preferred as *mamluk*s. Instead of being discriminated against because of their slave origins, these Turkish *mamluk*s soon discriminated against the freeborn Kurds, especially in the army of Ayyubid Egypt, the largest and most powerful part of the Ayyubid 'family confederation'. Here, the Ayyubid sultan recruited *mamluk*s in increasing numbers, until the *mamluk* corps and senior *amir*s were second only to the sultan himself in power. Sultan al-Salih Ayyub of Egypt (1240–49) then tried to use his *mamluk* army to impose his authority upon the Ayyubid realms. To do this al-Salih purchased even more Turkish *mamluk*s than before, attempting to segregate them from the rest of his army by building fortified barracks on Roda island on the western side of Cairo. Here new recruits and soldiers were instilled with pride in their Turkish origins and their *mamluk* status.

Sabil public water source north of Cairo's Citadel. Dating from the mid-14th century, it is decorated with the heraldic motif of its sponsor, the Mamluk *Amir al-Kabir* Sayf al-Din Shaykhu al-Nasiri. (Author's photograph)

CHRONOLOGY

1244	The Ayyubid sultan of Egypt's *mamluk* army defeats a combined Crusader and Syrian Ayyubid army at the battle of La Forbie.
1249–50	King Louis IX of France crusades in Egypt but is defeated; the Ayyubid Sultan al-Salih Ayyub dies during this campaign and is succeeded by his son Turanshah; the *Bahriyah mamluk* regiment mutinies and kills Turanshah; al-Salih's widow Shajar al-Durr and her new husband, the senior *mamluk* officer al-Mu'izz Aybak, rule until 1257; al-Ashraf, the Ayyubid ruler of Damascus, remains nominal sultan of Egypt until 1254.
1257–58	Assassination of Aybak, and subsequently of Shajar al-Durr herself; Aybak's son, al-Mansur 'Ali, becomes sultan.
1258–59	Mongols destroy Baghdad then invade Syria; al-Muzaffar Qutuz becomes Mamluk sultan.
1260	Sultan Qutuz defeats the Mongols at 'Ayn Jalut; the Mongols evacuate Syria; Qutuz is assassinated and al-Zahir Baybars becomes sultan.
1261	The Mongols invade Syria but are defeated at Homs.
1262–71	Numerous Crusader-held castles and towns fall to the Mamluks; a war of espionage and raiding begins between the Mongols and Mamluks.
1271	Crusading Prince Edward of England unsuccessfully attempts joint operations with the Mongols.
1272	Baybars brings Nubia under Mamluk overlordship; the Mamluks defeat the Mongols at al-Bira.
1274	The Mamluks sack the capital of Armenian Cilicia.
1277	Baybars campaigns in Anatolia but dies in Damascus; his son al-Sa'id Baraka becomes sultan.
1279	Baraka is deposed; al-Mansur Qalawun becomes sultan.
1280–81	Mongols devastate Aleppo but are defeated at the second battle of Homs.
1280–85	Failed revolt of Sunkur al-Ashqar in Damascus.
1284	Failure of the Nile flood causes famine in Egypt.
1285	The Mamluks take Crusader Marqab.
1288–90	Unsuccessful Mamluk campaigns in Nubia.
1289	The Mamluks take Crusader Tripoli.
1290–91	Qalawun is succeeded by his son al-Ashraf Khalil who takes Crusader-held Acre.
1293	Unsuccessful campaign by Sultan al-Ashraf in Lebanon; he is assassinated and al-Nasir Muhammad becomes sultan for the first time.
1294	Deposition of al-Nasir; Kitbugha Zayn al-Din becomes sultan.
1295 and 1296	Famines in Egypt.
1296	Massive desertion from the Mongols to the Mamluks; deposition of Kitbugha; Lajin al-Ashqar becomes sultan.
1298	Desertion of some Kipchaq and Mamluk *amir*s to the Mongols; assassination of Lajin; al-Nasir becomes sultan for the second time.

1299–1300	Mongol Il-Khan Ghazan invades Syria and defeats the Mamluks at Wadi al-Khazindar but Mamluk resistance causes Ghazan to withdraw.
1301–02	Mamluk punitive expeditions to southern Egypt.
1303	Ghazan's final invasion of Syria is defeated at Marj al-Suffar.
1309	Abdication of al-Nasir; Baybars al-Jashnakir becomes sultan.
1310	Al-Nasir becomes sultan for the third time.
1315	Sultan al-Nasir redistributes 'iqta fiefs.
1321–22	Serious disturbances between Christians and Muslims in Egypt; the Mamluks invade Cilician Armenia.
1325–26	Abortive Mamluk expedition to Yemen.
1335	Famine in Egypt.
1336–37	The Mamluks invade Cilician Armenia.
1341	Death of Sultan al-Nasir Muhammad.
1341–82	Al-Nasir's sons and grandsons used as puppet sultans by Mamluk military cliques.
1347	The Black Death reaches the Middle East.
1365	King Peter of Cyprus sacks Alexandria.
1382	Al-Nasir's grandson al-Mansur Hajji deposed; Barquq al-Yalbughawi becomes sultan for the first time.
1389–90	Barquq overthrown (1389) but regains the throne for the second time (1390).
1394	Confrontation between Barquq and Timur-i Lang.
1399	Death of Sultan Barquq; al-Nasir Faraj becomes sultan aged 13.
1400	Timur-i Lang sacks Aleppo and Damascus.
1405	Death of Timur-i Lang.
1405	Al-Nasir Faraj is deposed but regains the throne.
1412	Assassination of al-Faraj; al-Mu'ayyad Shaykh becomes sultan.
1415–18	Abortive rebellion by the Mamluk na'ibs of Damascus.
1419	The Mamluks annex Eregli, Tarsus and Adana in southern Anatolia.
1419	Plague in the Mamluk Sultanate.
1421	Death of al-Mu'ayyad Shaykh; his son al-Muzaffar Ahmad II becomes sultan but is replaced by al-Zahir Tatar who is himself replaced by his son al-Salih Muhammad.
1422	Al-Ashraf Barsbay becomes sultan.
1425–26	Mamluks occupy the Arabian port of Jidda; first Mamluk assault upon Cyprus captures King Janus at the battle of Khirokitia.
1429	Mutiny by the sultan's *mamluk* recruits.
1433	Unsuccessful Mamluk siege of Amid (Diyarbakir).
1438	Death of al-Ashraf Barsbay; his son al-Aziz Yusuf becomes sultan but is replaced by al-Zahir Jaqmaq.
1441–44	Unsuccessful Mamluk assaults upon Hospitaller-ruled Rhodes.
1453	Al-Mansur 'Uthman becomes sultan but is deposed by al-Ashraf Inal; plague further undermines the Mamluk Sultanate.
1460	Rioting by *mamluk* recruits; a Mamluk fleet and army accompany the Cypriot pretender Prince James to Cyprus.
1461	Death of al-Ashraf Inal; his son Ahmad III becomes sultan

1463	but is deposed in favour of al-Zahir Khushqadam. Mamluk army returns from Cyprus.
1467	Part of Syria is lost to the Dulghadir ruler Shah Suwar; death of Sulan al-Zahir Khushqadam; al-Zahir Yalbay becomes sultan but is overthrown in favour of al-Zahir Timurbugha.
1468	Al-Zahir Timurbugha is overthrown and al-Malik al-Ashraf Qayit Bay becomes sultan; the Mamluks are again defeated by the Dulghadir ruler, Shah Suwar.
1468–96	Al-Ashraf Qayit Bay defeats Shah Suwar, crushes Arab *bedu* revolts in Egypt and Syria, and defeats the Ottomans in a prolonged border war.
1496	Death of Qayit Bay; his son al-Nasir Muhammad becomes sultan.
1497–98	Portuguese explorers round Cape Horn and enter the Indian Ocean; assassination of al-Nasir Muhammad; al-Zahir Qansawh becomes sultan.
1500–01	Deposition of Qansawh; al-Ashraf Janbulat becomes sultan but is replaced by al-'Adil Tuman Bay who is then deposed in favour of al-Ashraf Qansawh II al-Ghawri.
1501	Sultan al-Ghawri reforms the Mamluk army with an increasing use of firearms; the Mamluk fleet defeats the Portuguese in the Red Sea.
1504–14	Shi'a Muslim Safavids from Iran and Iraq raid Mamluk and Ottoman Mamluk territory but are defeated by Ottoman Sultan Selim at Chaldiran (1514).
1506–09	Portuguese maritime campaigns block Mamluk trade in the Indian Ocean; combined Muslim fleets are defeated by the Portuguese off Gujerat.
1510	The Mamluk fleet is destroyed by the Hospitaller Knights of Rhodes near Ayas.
1514–15	The sultan's *mamluk*s mutiny in Aleppo; The Ottoman Sultan Selim destroys the 'buffer state' of Dhughadir.
1516	Sultan al-Ghawri establishes an anti-Ottoman alliance with the Safavids; the Mamluks are defeated by the Ottomans at Marj Dabiq where al-Ghawri dies; al-Ashraf Tuman Bay II becomes sultan.
1517	Ottoman Sultan Selim defeats Tuman Bay II at the battle of Raydaniya, ending the Mamluk Sultanate; Tuman and many Mamluk *amir*s are executed.

RECRUITMENT

In earlier centuries most slaves from the Eurasian steppes, including military recruits, entered the Islamic world via Khurasan in north-eastern Iran. However, this may already have been changing before the Mongol invasion overwhelmed the eastern Islamic world in the mid-13th century. The Muslim Volga Khanate on the northern edge of the steppes already played a major role in the slave trade, which suggested that many 'slave recruits' already came from non-Turkish Finno-Ugric peoples north of the steppes.

Fifteenth- to early 16th-century broken tip of a composite bow, with a notch to hold the bowstring, from the Citadel of Damascus. (IFPO; Patrick Godeau photograph)

Further west, the Russian city of Kiev played a similarly significant role as the northern terminal of three separate slave-trade routes across the western steppes. These western steppes were inhabited and ruled by Kipchaq Turks who exported slaves through Byzantine- and then Venetian-dominated Crimean ports.

This trading pattern was brutally interrupted by the Mongol conquest, which in turn made greater numbers of slave recruits available as a result of increased tribal fighting over diminished resources, significant population displacement and famine. Many *mamluk*s were enslaved captives or kidnap victims while others seem to have been sold by their own starving, impoverished parents. Turks, who had previously been expensive as *mamluk* recruits, became abundant. Despite this, they remained a military elite, and this elite status was perhaps reinforced by the possibility that some were members of what had been aristocratic clans that had lost status with the collapse of the Kipchaq state.

The increasing importance of routes across the western steppes and Black Sea may have made it easier for the last Ayyubid rulers and early Mamluk sultans to acquire *mamluk* recruits. That said, these western routes were not problem free. Initially, many recruits had been taken from the Crimea or Caucasus to what is now northern Turkey. From there they crossed Anatolia and then went by sea to Egypt or direct to Syria. From the middle of the 13th century, however, Mongol invasions in Anatolia interrupted this route.

Wakala hostel for merchants built by one of the last Mamluk sultans, al-Ashraf Qansawh II al-Ghawri in 1504–5. (Author's photograph)

The most obvious alternative was already available – namely a longer sea route across the Black Sea, past Constantinople to the eastern Mediterranean via the Aegean. The Mamluk Sultanate, therefore, formed an alliance with the Mongol Golden Horde, which by that time dominated the eastern Eurasian steppes, against the Mongol Il-Khanids of Iran and Iraq. Meanwhile, the fall of the Crusader 'Latin Empire of Constantinople' and its return to Byzantine rule in 1261 encouraged a three-way alliance between the Mamluks, the Golden Horde and a revived Byzantine Empire. The Italian maritime republic of Genoa, which had close links to Byzantium, soon formed an unofficial fourth member of this alliance, providing a maritime link between the Golden Horde and the Mamluk Sultanate.

Further changes came with the collapse of the Il-Khanate in the mid-14th century, by which time

the majority of *mamluk* recruits were probably taken from the Crimea in Genoese ships to Sinop or Samsun and onwards overland. The Mamluk Sultanate was geographically close enough to influence events in Anatolia but not to influence the Golden Horde itself. All that sultans in Cairo could do was conduct active diplomacy, sending ambassadors and occasional valuable gifts including military equipment. However, even the collapse of the Golden Horde in the latter part of the 14th century may have been but briefly beneficial, as it led to a resurgence of tribal warfare and perhaps made even more recruits available as *mamluk*s.

Elsewhere, however, the sultanate's main sources of recruits were under pressure because of the rising power of the Ottoman Turks. Following the Ottoman conquest of Constantinople in 1453, Sultan Mehmet the Conqueror banned Venetian and Genoese ships from transporting slaves from the Eurasian steppes through the Bosphorus and Dardanelles. Within a few decades this had a serious impact upon the Mamluk army, as did problems with the spice trade which undermined the sultanate's ability to pay for suitable recruits.

When the system was working properly it followed a relatively consistent pattern. A slave merchant, sometimes called a *khawaja*, was the recruit's first 'master'. In addition to bringing the recruits into the Islamic world a *khawaja* assessed an individual's potential and thus value. The most important military slave market was in, or near, the Cairo Citadel barracks or *tabaq* (pl. *tabaqah*). There were others in Damascus, and at the very end of the Mamluk Sultanate a new *tabaqah* and barracks was even established by Sultan Qansawh near the Khan al-Khalili market in central Cairo.

Very little else is known about such markets and barracks but it is reasonably clear that slave recruits were not mistreated – in fact rather the reverse, since they were a highly valuable 'commodity'. Surviving evidence shows that the price of recruits was always high, but could vary considerably.

'Arrival of the Venetian Ambassadors in Damascus', on a late 15th- or early 16th-century Venetian panel painting attributed to the school of Bellini. The costumes and architecture are so accurately portrayed that the artist must have been working from sketches made in the Mamluk realm. (Louvre Mus., inv. 1157, RMN, Paris)

For example, Sultan Qalawun is said to have been nicknamed *al-Alfi* 'the Thousander' because Sultan al-Malik al-Salih bought him as a Kipchaq slave for a 1,000 *dinars*, a huge sum of money. Over two centuries later the average price of a *mamluk* slave recruit was from 50 to 70 *dinars*, though some men cost a great deal more. Genoese mercantile records occasionally mention the selling price of slaves in the Crimea, though these seem to have been domestic servants, including an Abkhazian named Seniarius aged 18 to 20 who cost 470 *baricat aspers* (small coinage circulating in the eastern Mediterranean from the 12th to the 17th century), a 'white' Abkhazian named Coxani aged around 11 for 470 *baricat aspers*, another Abkhazian named Jacobus aged 5 for 175 *baricat aspers* and a female Abkhazian named Bruneta aged about 8 for 200 *baricat aspers*. Meanwhile, a 'black' slave from India called Arona, who was 14 to16 years old, sold for 640 *baricat aspers*.

Abkhazia is a Black Sea coastal region at the northern end of the Caucasus mountains and it was clearly a major source or transit area for non-Turkish slaves. *Mamluks* from this cultural background would have been included amongst those known as Circassians. Though regarded as secondary when compared to the preferred Turks, they had long been enlisted as military recruits and soon become prominent in the *Burji* (Tower or Citadel) regiment. Most probably arrived as Christians and also included Russians and Alans.

 ARMS AND ARMOUR OF THE 13TH AND 14TH CENTURIES
(For details of the archery equipment see Warrior 10: *Saracen Faris 1050–1250*).
(**1**) Mamluk *'askari* wearing laminated leather 'hoop armour' and a leather helmet. The thigh defences are based upon pictorial sources because there is not yet archaeological evidence for this form of armour.
(**2a**) The structure of a laminated leather cuirass based upon elements from several incomplete cuirasses.
(**2b**) The system of straps inside the cuirass which support the horizontal lames, showing how the straps go through to the exterior of the lowest lame.
(**3a**) The structure of a rawhide lamellar cuirass, based on the remains of two examples found in a tower of the Citadel of Damascus.
(**3b**) A single lamel showing the shaping of the upper and left edges when viewed from the front, but without any lacing.
(**3c**) External view of the lamellae overlapping upwards and to the left, with visible lacing.
(**3d**) Interior of the vertical edge of the lamellae showing the edging strip secured by rivets and additional lacing.
(**3e**) Attachment point for tassets, which are not included in this reconstruction.
(**4a**) Laminated leather helmet, based upon several examples found in a tower of the Citadel of Damascus. Part of the side is cut away to show (from outside to inside): the outer layer of gesso painted with several layers of orange-red varnish; a layer of pieces of roughly cut, thin cotton cloth, overlapping each other in irregular shapes; a middle layer of gesso; an inner layer of cloth; an inner layer of gesso; multiple layers of irregularly shaped, very thin leather and, finally, part of the interior. The dotted line indicates the complete outer profile.
(**4b**) Iron ring, shaped washer, and inner part of rivet beaten over to hold chin-strap.
(**4c**) Interior of the helmet showing soft leather supporting segments.
(**5**) Partially gilded iron mace head.
(**6a**) Straight-bladed sword with an almost rounded tip and a single broad fuller groove, gilded bronze pommel, leather-covered wooden grip, gilded bronze quillons and sleeve over much of the grip.
(**6b**) Wooden scabbard covered in dark shark-skin sleeves of light brown soft leather around scabbard beneath suspension points, polished or gilded bronze or brass collars for the rings which take straps to the belt, polished or gilded chape with extension up the lower side of the scabbard.
(**6c**) Leather belt with gilded bronze buckle, buckle-plate, strap-end and stiffeners.
(**6d**) One of a pair of gilded bronze loops for the scabbard suspension straps, attached to the back of the belt by short leather straps.
(**7a**) Dagger with gilded or polished bronze grip and guard.
(**7b**) Leather-covered wooden sheath with gilded or polished bronze mounts.

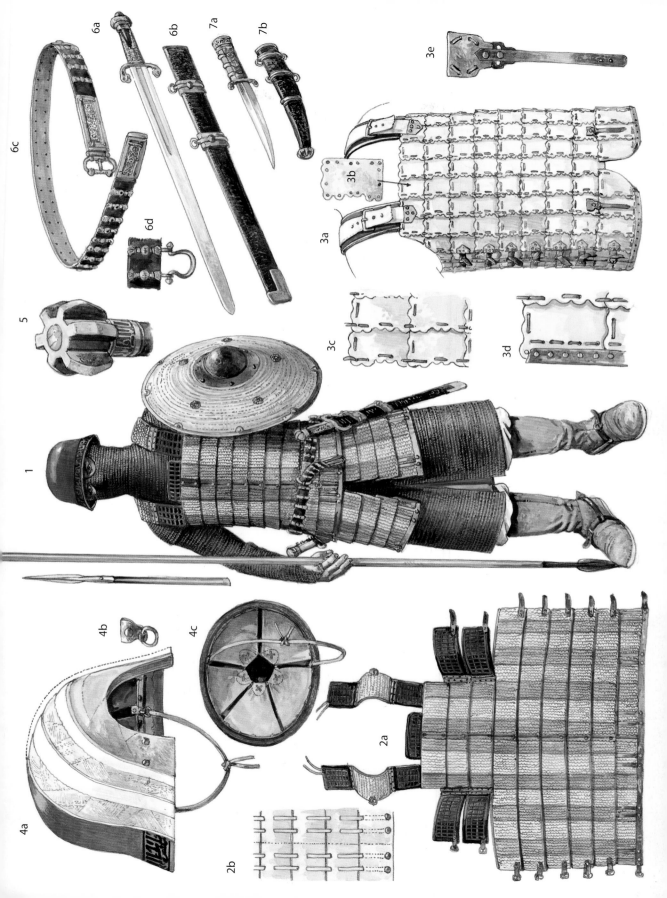

6a

6b

7a

7b

3e

6c

3b

3a

6d

5

3c

3d

1

4b

4a

4c

2a

2b

Delicately carved stone lintel in the largely Mamluk Shawbak castle in southern Jordan. (Author's photograph)

Slavery was widespread in parts of later medieval Russia, particularly in the expanding Principality of Muscovy, but whether this slavery was linked to a flourishing slave trade across the steppes remains unclear. Meanwhile, there was a legend that the ancestors of people from the 'eastern plains of [the] Circassian hills' included Ghassanid Christian Arabs who fled to Byzantium after the Muslim conquest of Syria in the 7th century. Perhaps this rumour was encouraged in an attempt to raise the prestige of Circassian recruits. Rivalry between Turkish and Circassian *mamluks* caused serious problems, indiscipline and rioting. Indeed there was a Circassian takeover of the Mamluk Sultanate from their Turkish rivals in 1382, though this quasi-dynastic change was also a result of several other factors.

Despite the large numbers of 'Crusader' prisoners of war who fell into Muslim hands during the 13th century, they rarely became *mamluks*. Instead, they were employed in construction work, both military and religious. There is, for example, strong evidence that captured Crusaders helped build the Citadel of Cairo, while their descendants worked on the dykes that controlled the Nile floods in the 1370s.

Meanwhile, Muslim victories brought new European prisoners of war to the Mamluk Sultanate. In addition to those captured by the *mamluks* themselves, small numbers also arrived as diplomatic gifts and these included some prisoners from the disastrous Crusader defeat outside Nicopolis in 1396. In 1420, the Italian traveller Emmanuel Piloti met some 200 French and Italian captives in Egypt. They had converted to Islam and had risen to prominence in the Mamluk army. Although such western recruits remained rare, they could

This silver-inlaid, late 13th- or early 14th-century Mamluk bronze basin known as the *Baptistère de Saint Louis* includes the best-known illustrations of Mamluk troops in this period, one of whom is in full armour. (Musée du Louvre, Paris; Author's photograph)

still be found at the end of the 15th century. In *The Pilgrimage of Arnold von Harff*, von Harff claimed to have met two boozy European *mamluks* in Cairo; one a Swiss named Conrad from Basle and the other a man from Denmark. As this late 15th-century work is seen as fiction by some scholars, though regarded as an account of a real journey by others, its reliability as a source can be questioned; however, the work certainly included accurate factual information.

Heraldic motif of the Mamluk *wazir* chief minister Sayf al-Din Manjak al-Silhadar 'the Sword-bearer', carved on the entrance to his palace in Cairo, built in 1346–47, and overlooking the *suq al-silah*, armourers' bazaar. It would originally have been painted. (Author's photograph)

Eunuchs formed a vital but specialized group amongst the *mamluks*. However, they were no longer as influential as they had been during the Fatimid and Ayyubid eras. Most are thought to have been of *Rumi* Byzantine Greek, *Habash* (Abyssian) Ethiopian, or *Hindi* Indian origin, while *Takrur* West African eunuchs were rarer, and most had been castrated before reaching Islamic territory. No eunuch seems to have reached the highest ranks and there were few amongst *amirs* of ten or *amirs* of 40. However, such men played an essential role in the military schools where *mamluk* recruits were educated.

Increasing problems with the recruitment of 'real' *mamluks* led to a variety of stopgap measures. Though the cultural ethos of the Mamluk Sultanate meant that significant reliance upon indigenous Syrians or Egyptians remained impossible, in the late 15th century an acute shortage of troops led some Damascus *amirs* to enlist the *zuwar*, quasi-military local 'gangs'. In 1499, the Mamluk governor of Damascus found himself so short of troops that he assumed authority over all 'black' slaves in the city, trained them as soldiers and formed them into military units which proved remarkably effective. A few years later the Mamluk sultan raised a force of handgunners, many of black African origin. However, they were away fighting the Portuguese in the Red Sea and Yemen when the Ottomans attacked in 1517, leaving only a small corps of North African and Turkoman arquebusiers to defend Egypt.

Naturally, it was only members of the upper echelons of Mamluk society whose personal careers were recorded. Perhaps the best known of these is Sultan Baybars al-Bunduqdari, whose life story became the stuff of legend in the Arab Middle East. The facts, as recorded, can be interpreted in a number of ways. Baybars was of Kipchaq origin. He and his fellows were enslaved as their clan, the Barli, were looking for security when the Kipchaq state collapsed in the aftermath of the Mongol invasion of southern Russia and the Ukraine. They headed either for the Crimea or to Wallachia where they put themselves under the protection of *khan* Awlaq (Vlach or Wallachian?) Anas. However, they were betrayed and some of the Barli children, including Baybars and a comrade named Baysari, were sold as slaves, eventually reaching Aleppo in Syria.

Another famous *mamluk* was Muhammad Ibn Mangli, who had a different story. This middle-ranking 14th-century *mamluk* officer was of Mongol origin and remembered how his father had been defeated, and himself captured, by the Mamluks. After going through the usual process of education and training as a *mamluk*, Ibn Mangli became an officer and then achieved more lasting fame as the writer of books on *furusiyah*, hunting, naval warfare and many other topics.

This inlaid bronze basin, with a similar date to the *Baptistère de Saint Louis*, has many combat and hunting scenes, including a Mamluk *'askari* wearing a helmet and lamellar cuirass. (Inv. 740-1898, Victoria & Albert Museum, London; author's photograph)

The belly of a mid-13th- to early 14th-century composite bow from Qal'at al-Rahba showing the wooden core, sinew binding and bone grip. (Qatar Museums Authority, Doha; author's photographs)

A 15th-century *mamluk* whose career is known in great detail is Qijmas al-Ishaqi, a *mushtarawat* 'purchased mamluk' of Sultan al-Zahir Jaqmaq (1438–53) who served in the *Zahiriyah* until the reign of Sultan al-Zahir Khushqadam (1461–67). Promoted to the rank of *amir* of ten by al-Zahir Yalbay in 1467, he developed close political links with al-Ashraf Qayit Bay before the latter became sultan (1468–96). During this period he became *Amir Khazindar* in charge of the Treasury and was governor of Alexandria from 1470 to 1478. Qijmas al-Ishaqi was also an *amir* of 100 in Egypt in 1472–80, was *Amir Akhur Kabir* from 1475 to 1480 and was *Amir al-Hajj* in charge of the annual pilgrimage to Mecca in 1479. Finally, promoted to the position of *na'ib*, or governor, of Damascus in 1480, he died there eight years later. During this illustrious career the pious Qijmas sponsored the construction of religious and charitable buildings in Alexandria, Cairo and Damascus, as well as the renovation of existing ones.

However, like so many *mamluks*, Qijmas also tried to ensure his own and his family's financial future. Even as an ordinary soldier of the *khassakiyah* regiment he established a 'self-benefitting' *waqf*, or religiously guaranteed endowment, in 1465. This consisted of two urban properties in Cairo and a plot of land in the Egyptian countryside. He reserved three-quarters for himself and his male descendants and one quarter for two of his own *mamluks* named Barsbay and Dawlatbay. Part of the annual revenues was shared between Koran reciters at the al-Azhar Mosque-university and the poor in the Muslim holy city of Medina. Other *waqf* endowments followed later in his career, including valuable sugar cane presses, orchards and rights to irrigation water. Qijmas al-Ishaqi had been a loyal supporter, so Sultan Qayit Bay endowed further *waqfs* for Qijmas and his descendants giving a clear example of how the Mamluk rulers rewarded their allies within the *mamluk* elite.

It has been suggested that the ties between some *mamluks* were genuine blood relationships, as they had been sold by their own families as young siblings who were not then separated by their new owners. Most *mamluks* would have lost contact with their original families – but not all. In the later 14th and the 15th centuries it became common for *mamluks* who reached the rank of sultan or senior *amir* to summon substantial numbers of their families from their original homelands. This had also been done on a smaller scale in earlier decades, and perhaps others would have done so if they had the power. What is clear is that supposedly 'slave' recruits to the *mamluk* ranks retained contact with their roots.

ORGANIZATION

A fundamental difference between the Mamluk Sultanate and the Ayyubid 'family federation' which it replaced was that power now became more concentrated in the capital, Cairo. Nevertheless, from the 14th century onwards the loyalty of major provincial *na'ibs* could not always be taken for granted. Perhaps to counter this possibility, major provincial centres such as Damascus and Aleppo had two *na'ibs*, one for the city and another for its citadel. Regional fragmentation increased as the power of the Mamluk central government declined and this was particularly apparent in frontier regions where most of the populations were nomadic Turkoman or Bedouin Arab tribes.

To some extent this decline reflected the efficiency and the size of the Mamluk army. Mamluk numbers were almost invariably exaggerated by their foes and even today there is a tendency to overstate the size of Mamluk armies. Furthermore, the numbers of fully trained, equipped and paid professional *mamluk* soldiers was always small and they normally formed a small proportion of field armies. When an army did consist primarily of *mamluks*, it tended to be a specialist force sent to conduct a focused campaign involving speed of movement and few, if any, sieges.

Exterior of the Bayt al-Ijani, a late 15th-century Mamluk palace, or great house, decorated with striped stonework in the old city of Damascus. (Author's photograph)

Massive wooden door leading into the courtyard of the Bayt al-Ijani, incorporating a smaller door for pedestrians. (Author's photograph)

On other occasions the *mamluks* were accompanied by substantial numbers of second-line troops and untrained volunteers, but even then the numbers were not particularly large. In the early decades of the Mamluk Sultanate a total of 40,000 to 50,000 soldiers, excluding auxiliaries, was normal. Of these, *mamluks* numbered around 4,000 in the days of Baybars I (1260–77), rising to 6,000 or 7,000 under Qalawun (1279–90), who himself had a personal corps of around 2,000 'ruler's' *mamluks* led by some 40 *amirs*. A European intelligence report called the *Devise des Chemins Babiloine*, which was probably based on a Mamluk administrative source, offered a detailed breakdown of the sultanate's strength. It summarized with the statement that, including both *mamluks* and other troops: 'The ... total of the power of the sultan in Babylon (Cairo) and Syria is 24,600 men, of which at least 15,000 are so poor that they can hardly maintain their horses'.[1]

Other evidence indicates than a senior late 13th- or early 14th-century *amir* could have a military household of 300 to 800 *mamluks*. In a 1315 *rawk*, or official military survey, there were 24 '*amirs* of 100', 12 from corps named after the rulers who raised them. The others were either the sons of *amirs* (, and as such not strictly *mamluks*) Mongol deserters from the Il-Khanate, or were of unknown origin. This survey then stated that, when reviewed, the strength of the army in Egypt also included 12,400 *mamluks* of *amirs*, 13,000 *mamluks* of provincial governors and 9,000 freeborn *halqa* troops. By the late 14th century numbers had dropped further, Sultan Barquq having only 2,000 to 3,000 'royal' *mamluks*, though in the early 15th century Sultan al-Mu'ayyad had between 5,500 and 5,700.

Medieval European visitors were often surprised to see almost no-one carrying weapons. Even soldiers normally only carried a small knife and, according to the Egyptian chronicler al-Qalqashandi, only the sultan's personal retinue carried swords at all times. This was the result of long-established and strictly enforced regulations. Around 1280 the *tadhkira*, or book on government and administration, written by Ibn al-Mukarram highlighted the authorities' wish to stop even some members of the Arab aristocracy obtaining weapons as they were not members of the *mamluk* elite.

The 'elite of the elite' were the *khassakiyah*, the trained and freed *mamluks* of the ruling sultan. They served in Cairo's Citadel as ceremonial guards, junior military secretaries and pages while receiving further training and making the contacts essential for senior promotion. In fact, very few *mamluks* became *amirs* if they had not first been one of the *khassaki*. In the sultan's

---

1 Irwin, R., 'How Many Miles to Babylon? The *Devise des Chemis de Babiloine* Redated', in Barber, M. (ed.), *The Military Orders, Fighting for the Faith and Caring for the Sick*, Aldershot (1994) p.59.

palace four of the most trusted, and perhaps best-looking, *khassaki* served as the ruler's *silahdariya* 'arms-bearers'.

Many sultans came to the throne after having been senior *amirs* for some time, and thus having already recruited *mamluk* retinues, some of whom then became their sultan's *khassakiyah*. Qalawun, for example, served as a senior officer for longer than his predecessor Baybars, and thus came to the throne with a significantly larger military household, though only 40 became *khassaki*. When a sultan died or was deposed, his *khassakiyah* were demoted, at least in terms of their influence, to become *qarani*. They also had to find a new leader and were thus included amongst the *mustakhdamun* who, for whatever reasons, had been obliged to transfer their allegiance to a new leader though they normally remained together as units.

The ranking system of the Mamluk army was relatively simple with *amirs* of ten, 100 and 1,000. However, it is unlikely that the two higher ranks normally had that number of fully trained *mamluks* under their command. In fact, evidence suggests that the overall ratio of men to officers in *mamluk* units was around 50 to one. Another system of ranking consisted of titles reflecting the role an individual *amir* performed, many of which were administrative, and in some cases seemingly ceremonial. The senior ranks were perhaps more complex as administrative roles connected with the army almost invariably went to military 'Men of the Sword' rather than the civilian 'Men of the Pen' who had earlier taken them. Given the abundance of such bureaucratic roles by the later 15th century, some scholars have questioned whether the upper echelons of the Mamluk Sultanate were still a real military elite. Certainly, their attitudes had more in common with modern corporate businessmen than with 'medieval warriors', and great emphasis was placed upon age, experience and promotion through dead men's shoes.

For ordinary *mamluks* – when not on campaign or training in the *maydan* – the main concerns were with where they were garrisoned and how close their units were to the centre of patronage in Cairo. Generally speaking, the greater the distance from the sultan, the lower the prestige of the troops in question, though of course those on the frontier played a vital role and could not be allowed to become disaffected. The *mamluks* also had a strong

Internal courtyard of the Bayt al-Ijani, with coloured stonework typical of this period. (Author's photograph)

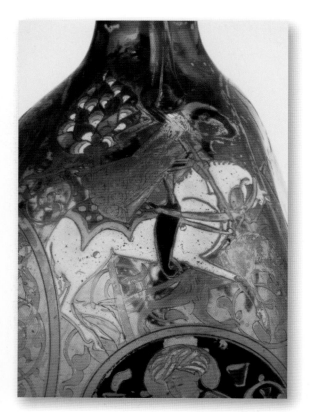

Mounted crossbowman hunting a lion, on an enamelled glass bottle made in Syria around 1260. (Inv. 69.1-20.3, British Museum, London)

prejudice about being stationed on the coast, as the presence of the sea was regarded as 'harming the army' because it was apparently harder to maintain discipline and carry out necessary training. The coastal defences were, therefore, usually garrisoned by low-grade, non-*mamluk* troops, and when Cyprus was briefly under Mamluk rule in the 15th century its garrisons were usually drawn from units that were currently out of favour in Cairo.

The traditional military structures of the medieval Islamic world were intended to keep professional soldiers close to the ruler. Hence the *'iqta* system supposedly meant that all ranks received sufficient reward to maintain military effectiveness and loyalty. *'Iqta* fiefs were allocated to those of senior or sometimes middle rank. These men were called *muqtas*. In the Mamluk Sultanate a *muqta* maintained a certain number of soldiers, his own *mamluks* and sometimes other lesser troops. He and his military household then owed military service to the sultan. The *muqta* also paid his troops' expenses from the revenues of his *'iqta*. The men would then purchase what they required on campaign from the *suq al-'askar* 'soldiers' market'. Each regular soldier was also paid, either by his *muqta* or by the sultan. If a *muqta* was disgraced, he was likely to lose his *'iqta*, and a fief was also cancelled in cases of illness or old age, though in these instances it would normally be replaced by a monetary pension.

For rank-and-file *mamluks*, military salaries were their main sources of income and it is clear that throughout the medieval period, military wages were almost always above those earned by skilled craftsmen. In the Mamluk Sultanate the entire economy seemed primarily designed to maintain the army. The process was well described in a handbook of administration written by Ibn al-Mukarram around 1280:

> The dues of amirs, Bahri mamluks, and Halqa al-Mansura, and jund [the rest of the army] must be collected in their names and remitted to their agents or deputies. Receipts bearing their signatures must be obtained from the agents confirming the amounts cashed in dirhams [the basic coinage] or the produce [non-monetary allowances] delivered to them. They [the agents or deputies] need not complain to their absentee clients about delays in remittance of the dues, and this matter must be settled without procrastination.[2]

The actual sums are difficult to translate into modern terms, yet the numbers do indicate large variations in pay between different ranks and between *mamluks* and lower-status troops. For example, in the early Mamluk period, the *ajnad al-halqa*, who were non-*mamluk* troops, received fiefs worth 10,000

---

2 Fernandes, L., 'On Conducting the Affairs of State: A Guideline of the Fourteenth Century', *Annales Islamologiques*, 24 (1988) p.88.

to 30,000 *dirhams* (500–1,500 *dinars*) per year, but at end of the 13th century Sultan Lajin reduced this to 250 to 1,000 *dinars* per year. In contrast the payment of *khassakiyah* 'royal *mamluks*' increased. In the early 14th century the lowest ranking *mamluk amir* was supposed to have an *'iqta* worth ten to 30 *dinars* a month, an *amir* of ten an *'iqta* worth 44 to 130 *dinars* a month, and an *amir* of 40 an *'iqta* worth 300 to 570 *dinars* a month. During the first half of the 15th century junior *mamluks* still only got 36 to 120 *dinars* a year whereas a senior *amir* would receive 500 to 700 *dinars* per year from their *'iqtas*, plus additional monthly payments of six or seven *dinars*.

An illustration from a Mamluk copy of *Sulwan al-Muta'* shows a ruler's attendants ready for the hunt and wearing typical Mamluk costume. (Homaizi Collection, Kuwait)

Other regular allowances were just as important to the ordinary *mamluk* and he received help with clothing as well as rations of meat which many exchanged for money, around eight *dinars* a month. Before each campaign *amirs* and their men usually received a special allowance known as a *nafaqat al-safar* in addition to their normal pay. It was to ensure that their equipment was in good condition and to buy any supplies they needed. *Mamluk* soldiers also got horses, camels and forage for their animals though the process for distributing horses is not entirely clear. For example, Sultan Qalawun distributed money to his *mamluks* to buy horses for upcoming campaigns, though these may have been additional or baggage animals.

The sultan gave his senior *amirs* horses twice a year, though not perhaps every year. Otherwise, *mamluks* are known to have been given a horse on completion of their training as part of the process by which they 'passed out' as freed *'askaris*. However, they only received replacements if they could prove that their previous mount had died or been killed. Some *mamluks* – perhaps only officers – also purchased *jana'ib* (sing. *janib*) or spare remounts before or during a campaign, and it is clear that *mamluk* cavalry armies had fewer remounts than had Mongol forces.

Many scholars have looked at the question of *mamluk* cavalry horses but until recently this has been almost solely on the basis of documentary evidence. Overall, the evidence strongly suggests that *mamluk* cavalry mounts were smaller than later medieval European 'knightly' horses – though this difference should not be exaggerated. It is also generally agreed that *mamluk* cavalry mounts were larger and better fed than those of ordinary Mongol tribal troops. More significant was the different style of horse harness used in the Mamluk Sultanate. It was similar to that used by the Eurasian steppe peoples and, in fact, the history of the horse harness in the steppe regions suggests strong, mutual influences between China and the Islamic world over many centuries.

Valuable horses required good stables and perhaps the most important of these was in the Citadel of Cairo. According to Doris Behrens-Abouseif, they were outside the main fortified enclosure, though connected to it, and were protected to the north-east by the slope of the steep Muqattam Hill: 'During

Interior of the eastern wall of the Citadel of Damascus, largely dating from the early 13th century. It includes large chambers that were used as barracks, workshops and storage rooms throughout the Mamluk period. (Author's photograph)

times of peace the connection was open; in times of insecurity, however, the Stables could be disconnected and access to the main part of the Citadel became far more difficult.'[3] The stables were also overlooked by the royal palace, as were the main *maydan* cavalry training area and principle horse market. From the later 14th century onwards, these stables became even more important. They acquired ceremonial functions and even had a *maq'ad* loggia where the sultan could hold audience, though this was only done in winter and early spring. In summer, such audiences took place in the *haws*, an open area higher up in the Citadel cooled by summer breezes.

Major *maydan* 'hippodrome' cavalry training grounds could similarly be used for ceremonial purposes and the most important in Cairo dated from the 9th century, long before the building of the Citadel. Destroyed by the first Mamluk Sultan Aybak, this huge *maydan* was restored by al-Nasir early in the 14th century. It was primarily intended as an arena for cavalry training. A raised chamber (*qasr*) would later be added to this *maydan*'s main gate and was linked to the Citadel by a private passage.

When al-Ghawri again restored the *maydan* at the start of the 16th century, it became a pleasure complex with an audience hall, a garden with aromatic imported trees hung with cages of exotic singing birds and an ornamental pool which could also be filled with flowers. The sultan even had a special bench with a velvet-covered seat, inlaid with ebony and ivory. Here he would sit in the shade of jasmine trees while attendant *mamluks* kept the insects away with their special fly whisks.

BELIEF AND BELONGING

Mamluk recruits did not start their careers as 'blank sheets' with no culture of their own. Most arrived as adolescents or young adults and it was inevitable that their cultural backgrounds would have an impact upon them as well as upon the Islamic society in which they found themselves.

During the early decades of the Mamluk Sultanate the largest group of recruits were of Kipchaq Turkish origin, the majority being adherents of the Tangrian shamanist faith, essentially the same as that of the Kipchaqs' Mongol conquerors. The Kipchaq state, which previously dominated most of the western steppes, had its own distinctive culture, several towns, some settled agriculture and extensive trade. There were, of course, other Turkic groups amongst the *mamluk* recruits, but it is unclear how much cultural difference there was between the various groups.

The *mamluk* training system inculcated adherence to Sunni Islam as the primary identity and the Mamluk Sultanate was emphatically Sunni

---

3 Behrens-Abouseif, D., 'The Citadel of Cairo: Stage for Mamluk Ceremonial', *Annales Islamologiques*, 24 (1988) pp.61–64.

(mainsteam Islam). Once educated and trained, *mamluk* soldiers found themselves part of a philosophical construct in which they represented the 'army of the day' and fought against the enemies of Islam while an 'army of the night' consisting of Muslim scholars and mystics 'fought' for Islam through prayer. Despite their occasionally unorthodox habits, especially a widespread consumption of alcohol, many of those *mamluks* whose careers brought them wealth and influence demonstrated their piety by sponsoring religious buildings and institutions whose domes and minarets still dominate the skyline of several Middle Eastern cities.

Where their relations with neighbouring states were concerned, it is clear that the *mamluks* regarded the remnants of the Crusader States as a minor problem. In contrast, the Mongol invaders and their Islamized Il-Khanid successors were seen as a mortal threat. Relations between the *mamluk* military class and indigenous Christians of the Middle East were not as relaxed as had existed in previous centuries, attitudes having hardened in the wake of the Crusades and the Christian 'reconquista' in Spain and Portugal. For the first time there was widespread persecution of Christian *dhimmis* or 'protected subjects' and conversion to Islam changed from a trickle to a flood.

Meanwhile, Muslim piety remained central to the legitimacy of the Mamluk Sultanate and the identity of ordinary *mamluks*. Naturally, the *Hajj*, the obligatory pilgrimage to Mecca, formed an essential part of this and Baybars is said to have been the first Mamluk sultan to send a camel with an elaborately decorated *mahmal* carrying a *kiswa* textile covering for the Kaaba in Mecca. Its departure was a very public religious and political

The fall of Crusader-held Tripoli to the Mamluks in 1289, by a late 13th- or early 14th-century Italian artist who had particularly accurate information about Mamluk costume and included the heraldic Lion of Baybars. (*Histoire Universelle*, Ms. Roy. 20.D.I, British Library, London)

The remarkable aqueduct that brought water from the Nile to the Citadel of Cairo was built in steps, each originally marked by a *saqiya* water-mill. It was re-activated in the first half of the 14th century to bring water to a Mamluk palace complex at the southern end of the citadel. (Author's photograph)

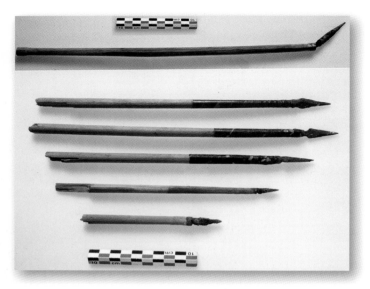

From the Citadel of Damascus, originating in the 15th to early 16th centuries – top to bottom: a crossbow bolt with a bolt head; the front parts of heads of four broken arrows; and the front part of a broken crossbow bolt. (IFPO; Patrick Godeau photograph)

gesture which other rulers would follow – it remained an Egyptian tradition that continued until the early 20th century.

Meanwhile, mainstream Sunni scholars tended to be suspicious of the increasing influence of *sufi* mystics. However, it is clear that the highly personal form of Islam that mystics offered found fertile ground amongst all ranks of the *mamluk* military class. The role of *sufis* in predicting Mamluk victories was also important in maintaining morale while stories about *sufis* whose personal power continued after their death confirmed the *mamluks'* belief that eternal life awaited martyrs. Therefore, soldiers should not fear death but should fight with an eye on a heavenly reward. Indeed, *mamluks* were often enthusiastic supporters of *sufi* movements and sponsored the building of their *khanaqah*, *tariqah* and *zawiya* meeting places, despite frequent criticism from more orthodox *'ulamma* religious leaders.

Another aspect of *mamluk* piety of which the orthodox religious establishment tended to disapprove was their veneration of relics such as the supposed swords of the Prophet Muhammad, the early *khalifs* and other Islamic military heroes to whom the *mamluks* could easily relate. The tombs, or supposed tombs, of early Muslim warriors in or around Palestine played a similar role. There were also thoroughly unorthodox locations, such as the place where blood from an early Islamic hero's wound stained a rock following a fight against the infidels.

C ## AN *AMIR* AT HOME

This wealthy home, dating from the later 15th century, was within the old city of Damascus.
(**1**) A high-ranking *amir* of eastern European Slav origin wears a thinly quilted cap, soft leather slippers, a cotton-lined linen shirt, and *sirwal* trousers of striped cotton fabric. His beard comb is cut from wood. The *kaftan* held by a female servant is a very loose-fitting garment with three-quarter length sleeves.
(**2**) The female servant, or domestic slave, wears a dress dating from the late 13th century.
(**3a**) The turban is kept in place using a pair of bronze hooks and a leather thong (late 13th century).
(**3b and 3c**) Large turbans for a high-status wearer (15th century).
(**3d**) Stiff leather cap (late 13th or 14th century).
(**3e**) Fur-lined, quilted cap (14th century).
(**3f**) Thinly padded, quilted cap (14th–15th centuries).
(**3g**) Characteristic *mamluk* fluffy *zamt* hat of white sheepskin dyed a strong red (14th–15th centuries).
(**3h**) Thinly padded, quilted cap with fur lining (14th–15th centuries).
(**3i**) Decorated leather purse (15th or early 16th century).
(**3j**) Small personal knife and sheath (13th–14th centuries).
(**3k and 3l**) Soft leather riding boots (late 13th–14th centuries).
(**3m**) Soft leather shoe (late 13th century).
(**3n**) Soft leather walking boot (late 13th century).
(**3o**) Leather sandals (13th–-4th centuries).

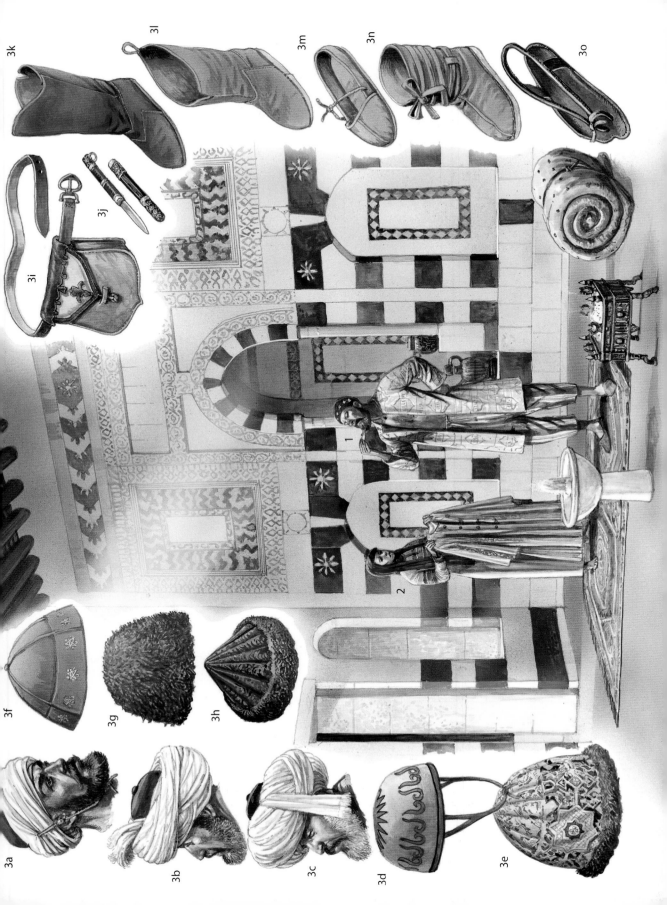

3k

3l

3m

3n

3o

3j

3i

3f

3g

3h

3a

3b

3c

3d

3e

1

2

The massive castle of al-Subayba on the southern foothills of Mount Hermon in the Israeli-occupied Golan Heights played a strategic role during the prolonged Mongol threat to Syria. Its Mamluk garrison was provided with excellent facilities, including latrines with flowing water, as shown here next to the castle's main entrance. (Author's photograph)

Like the Crusaders, many *mamluks* believed in help from good spirits or angels as well as the negative effect of evil spirits or demons. Visions and divine signs were important, as were the use of spells, talismans and written charms against demons or evil *jinn*. In Egypt there was also belief in the magical power of ancient carved statues, perhaps largely of pharaonic origin.

The somewhat unorthodox views of the *mamluk* elite were also demonstrated in their attitude towards death, burial and tombs. Unlike their Fatimid and Ayyubid predecessors, Mamluk rulers were not normally buried within their palace complexes and from the start of the Mamluk era it became established tradition for sultans to be buried in mausoleums attached to a religious foundation that they themselves had established.

In the great struggle against the last Crusader outposts, *mamluk* casualties were remarkably low while the elite's losses against the Mongols were much higher. Here it is worth noting that medieval Muslims appear to have had special reverence for the bodies of those who fell in battle against the infidels. As the Italian scholar Roberta Denaro recently pointed out at a colloquy in Cairo, special status was given to martyrs, who 'will not feel any pain when deadly wounded, immediately after his death he will be given a new body or, following some traditions, his soul will enter into a green bird; his corpse, if found, will be well preserved, smelling of musk'.[4]

In the 14th and 15th centuries the *mamluks* faced a terrifying new threat to which they were particularly exposed. The plague swept across their lands and it is clear that the *mamluk* class suffered more seriously than other sections of society. Newly arrived foreigners and children were hit worst because they had not built up the same immunities as the local population. In the epidemic of 1458–60 about one-third of registered *mamluks* died. The ruling sultan's *khassakiyah* suffering very badly because it consisted of younger soldiers than those in the *qarani* units raised by previous rulers whom, it seems, had acquired some local resistance. However, the impact of war and disease should not be exaggerated; by the later 15th century most of those *mamluks* whom we know about died of strokes, hernias, gout and other unwarlike ailments.

Discipline in the Mamluk army was based upon Islamic law yet for reasons which remain unknown, the venerable role of 'Qadi [judge] of the Army' disappeared during the Mamluk period. Punishments were usually physical, with public flogging and amputation for more serious offences being the norm. A particularly humiliating punishment was being tied to a frame on the back of a two-humped camel and paraded in public. However, this could be considered a lenient sentence when one considers that during the Mamluk period the very worst offenders were crucified on camelback.

4 Denaro, R., '"The Most Beautiful Body": The Role of the Body in Martyrdom Narratives' (IFPO Cairo 15–18 December 2011).

Few *mamluk amirs* got through their careers without some form of punishment. This was normally in the form of internal banishment while imprisonment was rare and usually for political reasons. Demotion, either of individuals or entire units, could also be used as a disciplinary measure.

The *sayfiya* were *mamluks* who served the sultan directly, following the death or dismissal of their previous officer. Their prestige and pay was somewhat low but they were considered politically harmless and could, therefore, be promoted on an individual basis.

The titles *tarkhan* and *battal* were sometimes given to discharged *mamluks*. *Tarkhans* tended to be respectable *mamluks* who had been pensioned off for reasons of age or health, while *battals* were more numerous than *tarkhans* and were often officers banished to a distant province. Rank-and-file *battals* had not been punished individually but as a unit. They could still serve in a crisis and so were not entirely excluded from the Mamluk military system. They were also employed in auxiliary duties in Cairo or to garrison seaports – a very unpopular posting.

There is no doubt that the *mamluks* developed a strong sense of 'class solidarity' but the idea that they had any sort of inferiority complex as 'ex-slaves become masters' is entirely wrong. In fact, prejudice against freeborn troops increased from the late 13th century onwards. Within the *mamluk* system *khushdashiyah*, or unit solidarity, was clearly important. It was apparent in the close bonds between *mamluks* and their original masters and their own senior *amirs*, and with each other. The Muslim scholar Ibn Taymiyah described the bonds of *khushdash* in the following terms: 'A person involved in such a tie is called a *sadiq* [friend] or a *rafiq* [companion] and in Turkish he is called *khushdash* [comrade].'

LEFT
Musicians playing *buq* large trumpets, large and small drums and small cymbals on a c.1315 Mamluk copy of the *Automata*. They are arrayed in front of a wall decorated with Mamluk heraldic motifs. (Free Gallery of Art, Washington)

RIGHT
Burj al-Sba, built by the Mamluks around 1475, is one of a chain of small fortresses along the vulnerable coast beneath the Lebanese city of Tripoli. (Author's photograph)

Fifteenth- to early 16th-century broken arrow butts and nocks from the Citadel of Damascus. (IFPO; Patrick Godeau photograph)

'The Army of Firuz' in an early 14th-century Mamluk copy of *Sulwan al-Muta' fi 'Udwan al-Atba'*. Although the Mamluks did not use war elephants, other aspects of military equipment in this manuscript illustration reflect those used in Egypt and Syria. (Homaizi Collection, Kuwait)

Amongst the *mamluks*, however, the loyalty of *khushdash* was not absolute, as it was more of a mutual understanding that included financial rewards. Furthermore, political instability, frequent changes of sultan and the occasional return of a sultan for two or even three reigns could cause serious difficulties between the *mamluks* of each ruler. Fortunately, *mamluk* rivalries involved little violent fighting and even when conflicts briefly spilled onto the streets, the ordinary people of Cairo were rarely involved. The only significant exceptions were the *harfush* 'rabble' of unemployed, semi-criminal underworld gangs. Many of these *ju'adiyyah* 'curly haired ones' lived on handouts from rival *mamluk* leaders and the nicknames given to some *amirs* perhaps reflected such food donations. For example, the great traveller Ibn Battuta recalled how one Mamluk *amir* named Tushtu was known as 'green chickpeas'. He not only endowed many charities but enjoyed great support amongst the *harfush* whom he organized into bands of vagabonds.

A communal way of life in barracks or large households presumably strengthened *khushdashiyah*. The *khassakiyah* 'royal *mamluks*' were almost entirely quartered within the Citadel of Cairo, close to the sultan, while the *amirs' mamluks* largely lived within the city of Cairo, in or near the large houses of their commanding *amir*. Similarly, *amirs* normally lived in the main cities of the Mamluk Sultanate and not on their *'iqta* estates. Cairo was the favoured location and several quarters still contain the remnants of the small palaces of powerful *amirs*. Restoration of these and other structures confirms the *mamluk* habit of decorating these buildings with their own heraldic motifs. Buildings from this period in Cairo, Damascus and elsewhere also show architectural influences from as far afield as Sicily, the Crusader States, Andalusia, Khurasan, Mongol Iran, Hospitaller Rhodes and even late medieval India.

Relatively little is known about *mamluk* home life. Recruits were probably not permitted to marry until they were freed on the completion of their training. However, it is clear that numerous Turkish women, both slave and free, and virtually all of adolescent age, arrived in the wake of Turkish recruits and this was presumably true of non-Turks as well. Indeed, *mamluks* normally married slave girls or the daughters of other *mamluks*.

Now and then surviving records shed further light on what might be called '*mamluk* marriage'. One such was entered into a chronicle because of its legal interest as it concerned a matrimonial dispute within Cairo's *mamluk* elite in 1470 when a young *mamluka* (female *mamluk*) filed a suit with the chief judge. When summoned to state her case: 'the youthful virgin bowed low, stating that she was poverty-stricken and weary of begging. Her parents had been absent [from the area of Cairo] for a period exceeding three years.' With no one else to do it for her, she therefore asked one of the magistrates to arrange a suitable marriage. Three men were recommended, of whom the girl chose a *khassaki* in the most prestigious *mamluk* corps. The judge stipulated that consummation must wait until the girl was older.

Unfortunately, the young soldier was then accused of forcing himself upon his young bride and then promptly divorcing her, apparently thinking he could get away with it because his officer was one of the sultan's guards. The people of the Bulaq quarter where the young bride lived rose up in her support and conveyed her to the residence of the *Dawadar al-Kabir* who was the soldier's *ustadh* (patron or officer). The *mamluk* confessed and was sentenced to a flogging, whereupon his officer loudly complained, only to be threatened with a flogging himself. Other members of the *mamluk* elite also tried to intercede on the soldier's behalf, suggesting that he merely pay a fine, whereupon the girl's local supporters again protested. It was then discovered that the soldier and his comrades had been bullying the people of Bulaq, stealing straw, animal fodder and chickens. In the end the ex-husband was flogged and the local people rejoiced at his public humiliation.[5]

Amongst the *mamluks*, elite life clearly became increasingly sophisticated, though this did not necessarily mean they were effete. For example, the use of scents became common amongst wealthy men and women, there already being a distinction between those considered suitable for women and those considered masculine, such as musk. Men who could afford to do so are known to have scented themselves before battle. The reason remains unclear but it may have been to maintain morale amidst the nauseating odours of combat, or perhaps it was a religious gesture and they were preparing their own corpses for martyrdom.

Few *mamluks* are thought to have become fluent in Arabic, with Kipchaq being used by Turkish and perhaps some Circassian *mamluks* as a common tongue. Furthermore, a written 'Mamluk Kipchaq' was not only used for some military training manuals but also had its own literature, including poetry. Somewhat different is a Mamluk version of the 11th-century Uigur Turkish *Kutadgu Bilig* 'Knowledge that Brings Wealth of Kingship', a mirrors-for-princes-style book of advice by the Central Asian Kara-Khanid Turkish scholar Yusuf Khass of Balasagun. There was also a Turkish abbreviation of the huge Persian *Shahnamah* epic poem, translated for Sultan Qansuh al-Ghuri then transcribed and illustrated for the sultan in 1511.

Where Arabic literature is concerned, the Mamluk period was a silver rather than a golden age. Much of the poetry is in the form of traditional

The fortifications of the Citadel of Aleppo largely date from the Ayyubid period but the monumental upper chamber above the inner gate on the left was added by the Mamluks. (Author's photograph)

5 Petry, C. F., 'Conjugal Rights versus Class Prerogatives: A Divorce Case in Mamluk Cairo', in Hambly, G. R. G. (ed.), *Women in the Medieval Islamic World: Power, Patronage, and Piety*, London (1998) pp.228–32.

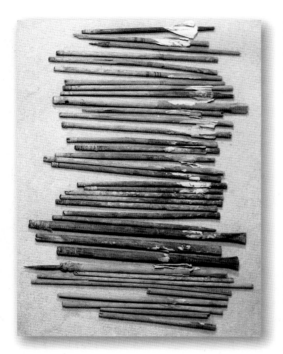

Mid-13th- to early 14th-century crossbow bolt shafts of various weights from Qal'at al-Rahba. Several have paper flights still attached and one has a slender armour-piercing bolt head. Also shown is one arrow for a hand-held bow (11th from the top) distinguished by the nock in its butt. (Qatar Museums Authority, Doha; author's photograph)

panegyrics of rulers which sound sycophantic and tedious to modern ears. One example praises the brief reign of Sultan al-Salih Isma'il (1342–45) and starts with the words:

In the name of God, the merciful, the compassionate.
Praise be to God, who mended the decay of the Islamic community
By the most powerful sultan, who made its face blossom and its eye smile.
(Praise be to God, who) Saved the case of the sultanic kingdom by
The firmest king, that delayed its death for its supporters
And that sped up its destruction of its enemies.[6]

In stark contrast, live theatrical and often vulgar performances called *khayal* were supposedly despised by the upper classes. The earliest known collection was assembled during the early Mamluk period by Ibn Daniyal (1248–1311) and one of their stock characters was the soldier tricked or trapped into an unsuitable marriage. Other public performers included sword swallowers and *bahlawan* 'champions' who included masters of one or more martial art. Fencers performed for 'pleasure seekers and loafers' while wrestling was particularly popular – Sultan al-Muzaffar Hajji (1346–47) shocked contemporaries by not merely enjoying such 'common sports' but even taking part, wearing the leather trousers of a professional wrestler.

Given the origins of most *mamluks*, and the increasing number of Europeans in their ranks in the later 15th century, it is hardly surprising that alcohol was widely drunk in private. There was also drug-taking, with the use of *banj* or hashish having spread during the 12th and 13th centuries. Hashish was much cheaper than wine in the 13th century and Muslim jurists of the Hanafi school of Islamic law declared it to be legal. In contrast, opium was much more expensive and only used by some members of the social elite, probably including wealthy *mamluks*.

APPEARANCE AND EQUIPMENT

Mamluks of the Ayyubid sultans wore their hair long, falling loosely to their shoulders, and this remained the case under the first Mamluk sultans. Al-Ashraf Khalil (1290–93) then ordered his *mamluks* to wear a small turban, a fashion which persisted until Sultan al-Nasir Muhammad had his own head shaved when he went on *Hajj* pilgrimage in 1332. This 'new look' was then promptly adopted by the rest of his household, including his *mamluks*.

Costume was clearly important in such a stratified society as that of the Mamluk Sultanate, but it was also subject to changing fashions. One quite

6   Van Steenbergen, J., 'Qalāwūnid Discourse, Elite Communication and the Mamluk Cultural Matrix,' *Journal of Arabic Literature*, 43 (2012) p.8.

dramatic change occurred during the rule of al-Zahir Barquq, the first of a new line of Circassian rather than Turkish sultans, who wanted to lower the status of the existing *mamluk* elite in favour of a new elite loyal to him. Other changes were localized, as when a governor of Qal'at al-Rum ordered his soldiers to dress, or arm themselves, like Mongols in order to frighten their foes. In contrast, Sultan al-Nasir shocked *mamluk* society by adopting Bedouin Arab costume, even wearing it in the courtly confines of Cairo Citadel in 1342.

The little fort at Aqaba in southern Jordan dates from the reign of Qansawh II al-Ghawri during the final years of the Mamluk Sultanate, and incorporates elements reflecting the adoption of firearms. (Author's photograph)

Detailed information on 15th-century *mamluk* costume was brought back to Europe by travellers such as Bertrandon de la Brocquière. Several times he had to adopt local dress, one such occasion being when he disguised himself as a *mamluk* to accompany a leading merchant. He purchased 'two ankle length white robes, a whole cloth headdress, a cloth girdle, a pair of fustian trousers to tuck my shirt into … [also] I had an overcoat of white silk covered with poplin which was very useful during the nights'.[7] In addition, he acquired a robe of light, white, waterproof felt and a decorated shield. Meanwhile, the 'Arabs', by whom Bertrandon probably meant local non-Turks, wore 'robes with great sleeves a foot and a half wide and much longer than their arms'.

As in so many cultures, headgear was a primary indicator of status amongst *mamluks*. It could also serve as a mark of high favour, as when a Mamluk sultan gave a brocade turban to a minor Ayyubid ruler in Syria, along with a 'robe of honour'. In the early Mamluk period the traditional *imama*, or Arab style of turban, was probably only worn by religious figures and not by soldiers. In later years, the *mamluks* themselves adopted various styles of turban, some of which became large and elaborate. Shape, material and colour provided information about the wearer, and Middle Eastern fashions were worn differently from those in North Africa. Bertrandon de la Brocquière described turbans that were large at the top, like those other 'Moors wear but which also hung down on both sides of the ears for the width of the cloth [of which the turban was made]'.

Initially, the sultan's turban, and perhaps those of very senior *mamluk amirs*, was called a *takhfifah* 'lighter one'. However, as headgear grew larger and more difficult to wear, *mamluks* adopted a *takhfifah saghirah* or 'small lighter one'. Sultan Barquq wore this smaller turban in public in 1394 but the fashion did not immediately catch on. Indeed, those who wore any type of *takhfifah* were sometimes criticized as 'careless' because this turban was 'inferior' to the tall *kallawtah* hat previously worn by *mamluks* beneath their turbans.

The stiffened and sometimes quilted *kallawtah* hat had been known since pre-Islamic times and had already undergone many changes. During the

7   De la Brocquière, Bertrandon (tr. G. R. Kline), *The Voyage d'Outremer by Bertrandon de la Brocquière*, New York (1988) p.36.

Ayyubid and early Mamluk periods, it was usually yellow though the textile covering could also be patterned. After the *mamluks* started shaving their heads in 1332, a *kallawtah* thrust firmly on the head allowed them to wear more elaborate turbans. Meanwhile, the fur-lined and originally Turkish *sharbush*, brought to Egypt by Saladin, was abolished in the later 14th century, and was replaced by the *zamt*, a fluffy woollen hat that became the badge of the *mamluk* military class.

Quilted textiles had an ancient history, right back to pre-Islamic Iran and India. During the Mamluk Sultanate, they became even more popular. A *tiraz* embroidered

Nihayat al-Su'l was one of the more original Mamluk military training texts. Here a cavalryman controls his horse with one hand while in the other he holds a sabre and large *daraqa* shield (seen from the side) raised high to protect himself from enemy arrows. (Add. Ms. 18866, f.130r, British Library, London; Abdulrahman Mostafa photograph)

panel on the upper sleeves of coats worn by ruling and military elites may also have had Iranian or Central Asian origins. Its inscription bore the ruler's name and it was supposedly worn only by those closest to the ruler. However, the *tiraz* may also have become merely decorative during the sultanate. Colours could proclaim identity, with yellow having been used by Ayyubid and early Mamluk sultans for flags and emblems, and red perhaps used as a secondary 'heraldic' colour. Certainly, yellow, gold and red were the colours most often mentioned in connection with diplomatic gifts of clothing, horse harness and flags.

The Mamluk Sultanate had a system of heraldry that was almost unique in the Islamic world. However, it was not used in the same way as European heraldry, and motifs were rarely handed down the generations. *Mamluk* heraldry was not intended to show an individual's family origins but usually indicated the role he played at the start of his career and, sometimes, his association with a particular patron. The main motifs thus included a horizontal bar identified with the *barid* courier system, a diamond which has been identified as a *buqja* napkin, a pellet bow, polo sticks and a cup.

HORSE HARNESS

(**1**) Reconstruction of a late 13th or early 14th century saddle from the Citadel of Damascus, partially uncovered to show its structure. The front of the pommel and rear of the cantle are covered in embossed and polished, but not colour-stained, leather and have a broad interlace pattern border and a central medallion containing confronted harpies.

(**2a**) Reconstruction of a highly decorated late 13th- or early 14th-century saddle from the Citadel of Damascus. The gesso surface covers, and to a substantial degree also shapes, the entire external surface of the saddle including the cantle, pommel and saddle boards. It is painted with transparent red-orange varnish which is decorated with an Arabesque pattern that is also cut into the surface of the gesso. There is an edging strip of black Arabic inscription and circular painted medallions of the 'Lion of Baybars'.

(**2b**) Rear view of the cantle of the saddle.

(**3a and 3b**) Front and side reconstructions of a 14th-century wood and ivory, or bone, stirrup.

(**4a**) A decorated 15th-century bridle and bit.

(**4b**) Close-up of decoration formed from short leather pendant straps to which gilded and embossed decorative copper plates are riveted.

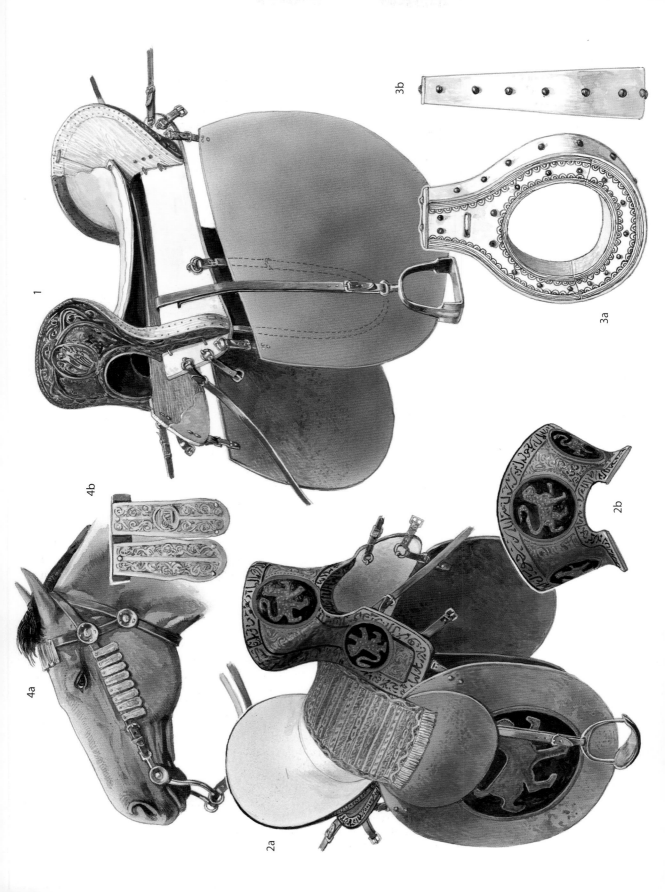

'Askaris were trained to use their weapons in a variety of ways. Here a late 15th-century Mamluk manuscript shows two-handed spear thrusting with shields worn over the upper arm and shoulder. (Keir Collection, London)

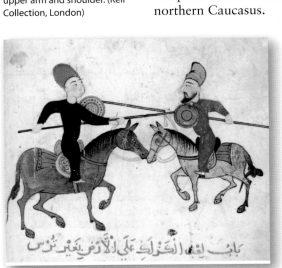

Michael Meinecke has calculated that several hundred variations on the basic heraldic theme would have been needed during the *mamluk* period. These variations were done by using different colours, multiplying the number of devices, and dividing the heraldic field upon which these motifs were placed. Therefore, it is not surprising that the single devices seen during the early Mamluk Sultanate evolved into a horizontally divided, tripartite field containing a variety of different devices.

In the last decades of the Mamluk period, a standard combination of six devices was adopted as a corporate blazon and by the 15th century the Mamluk ruling class placed their own personal heraldic designs on a remarkable array of objects to indicate ownership or the fact that a particular person had donated an object or building for charitable reasons. Heraldic designs were also added to diplomatic gifts and have been found not only on weapons in the western steppes but also on appliqué work textiles in the northern Caucasus.

Two further examples of appliqué textiles were found in a late *mamluk* arsenal, or workshop, in the Citadel of Damascus, one of which was an example of *mamluk* heraldry. As they did with so many other things, the Mamluk Sultanate inherited a system of military arsenals from their Ayyubid predecessors. A substantial part of their inventory later remained in place following the fall of the Mamluk Sultanate to the Ottomans and was mentioned in Ottoman records over a century later. European visitors occasionally also caught glimpses of their mouldering contents. On other occasions we learn about their contents because an enemy failed to find them. This happened in 1365 when a Crusader force from Cyprus briefly seized control of Alexandria but, according to the chronicler al-Nuwairi, the looters missed the arsenal, which contained 60,000 arrows as well as many bows, swords, spears, coats of mail, artillery, naptha, other war material and siege engines.

More recently, archaeologists have uncovered substantial fragments of what were almost certainly Mamluk arsenals and their associated workshops. For example, Syrian–French excavation at al-Rahba on the Euphrates in 1996 noted the presence of an area of such workshops near the castle. Carbon-dating of military material which probably came from al-Rahba spans the Ayyubid and early Mamluk periods, including a wood-lined 'hard hat' bearing the heraldic device of Sultan Baybars dating from around 1285. Another Syrian excavation at the castle of Masyaf uncovered fragments of Mamluk period 'arms and armour', details of which are so far unpublished. Such arsenals played a significant role during the final Mamluk siege of Crusader-held Acre in 1291 when the sultan ordered the governors of cities, provinces and castles to provide armour, as well as siege equipment, to be drawn from arsenals under their authority.

Major urban citadels had workshops within their walls, perhaps for repairs, or close by in the city for manufacture. Archaeology indicates the reuse and recycling of different sorts of material from leather straps to the iron elements of scale-lined cuirasses and arrowheads from damaged arrows. This was a 'waste not want not' culture, perhaps reflecting the Mamluk Sultanate's poverty in some raw materials, particularly metals. At times there was such a shortage of equipment and clothing that members of non-elite *halqa* shared the same hat and sword, swapping over before each man entered the presence of the *na'ib*, as happened in Damascus in 1392. *Mamluk* troops were not mentioned, so presumably they were given priority at this time of shortage. Over a century later in 1513 the Mamluk sultan gave to his own *khassikiyah* 800 helmets, 600 sets of horse armour, coats of mail and weapons from *mamluks* who had died during a recent plague, this equipment having presumably been returned to the arsenal.

Though the iron mines of Lebanon had been virtually exhausted, craftsmen still made high quality arms in Damascus. Those who produced real steel were closely supervised by the Mamluk authorities to stop cheating or a decline in standards. This system was described in an early 14th century legal treatise by Ibn al-Ukhwana who wrote that: 'An honest and trustworthy [person] from amongst them (the craftsmen) is chosen (as inspector). He prevents them from mixing steel needles with soft iron for, when sharpened, they (the fakes) may be taken for Damascus steel.'[8] The fate of the armourers who were forcibly transported from Damascus to Samarqand by Timur-i Lang featured prominently in an account written by the Spanish ambassador

Nocks and butts of fragmentary arrows from a building in the Citadel of Damascus, late 15th to early 16th centuries.
(1–4) Basic forms of nock seen amongst hundreds of arrow fragments.
(5–37) Colour schemes seen on the butts of 112 fragments. Grey represents bare wood. The number of examples are in brackets: 5 (2); 6 (3); 7 (1); 8 (1); 9 (1); 10 (1); 11 (10); 12 (2); 13 (19); 14 (2); 15 (2); 16 (2); 17 (6); 18 (2); 19 (7); 20 (1); 21 (2); 22 (4); 23 (2); 24 (2); 25 (10); 26 (2); 27 (2); 28 (1); 29 (1); 30 (13); 31 (1); 32 (1); 33 (1); 34 (2); 35 (3); 36 (2); 37 (1).

8 Hassan, A. Y. al-, 'Iron and Steel Technology in Medieval Arabic Sources', *Journal for the History of Arabic Science*, 2 (1978) p.39.

Clavijo following his visit to Timur's court in 1404: 'At one end of the city there is a castle … In this castle the lord has as many as a thousand captives, who were skilled workmen, and laboured all the year around at making armours and helmets, bows and arrows.'

Despite this loss of armourers, the industry survived in Damascus and a few decades later Bertrandon de la Brocquière recalled that he had to buy a sword and quiver secretly 'for, if the police had found out, those who had sold them to me would have been in danger'. The impact of Timur's abduction of so many craftsmen was a significant blow, but was not the only reason why the iron-starved Mamluk Sultanate tried to import equipment and raw materials during the 15th century. A European source recounting the fall of Jacques Coeur, the man credited with financing the French armies that expelled the English at the end of the Hundred Years' War, gives insight into the state of the industry at that time. In 1451 he was accused of shipping cuirasses, mail shirts and weapons such as guns and crossbows to the Mamluk Sultanate in return for exemption from customs dues when purchasing pepper. In his *Chronique de Charles VII*, Jean Chartier added that Coeur was also accused of sending armourers, perhaps to instruct *mamluk* craftsmen in the repair of European-style armour. This may strengthen the impression that the *mamluks* were still short of experienced armourers, perhaps as a lingering result of Timur-i Lang's invasion.

TRAINING AND CAMPAIGNING

There were clear variations in the standards of training between units, with the current ruler's *khassakiyah* being better than the *mamluks* of *amirs*. Nevertheless, a sultan who won the throne after a lengthy career as an *amir* had a longer time to train his men. Quite where the *mamluks* of previous

HORSE ARMOUR

(**1a**) Horse armour, late 13th to 14th centuries, consisting of three cloth-covered, scale-lined elements covering the rear, front and neck of the animal. Circular heraldic medallions made of appliqué work cloth are sewn to the covering of the armour. The horse's head is protected by an iron chamfron consisting of three hinged elements, covered with stained leather secured to the iron plates by a decorative system of lacing.

(**1b**) Detail of the structure of the corner of scale-lined horse armour with the decorative outer layer of cloth removed so that only the lowest three rows of riveted bronze scales are showing.

(**1c**) Interior of the corner of the scale-lined horse armour showing the main leather structural foundation, the large copper rivets securing the edging strip, the beaten heads of three of the four rivets holding each scale and the fourth rivet securing a scale that is not beaten flat but goes through a rectangular copper washer before being turned over.

(**1d**) Demonstration of the method of joining the sheets of horse armour beneath the animal's neck.

(**2a**) Laminated 15th-century leather horse armour consisting of five main elements to cover the rear, sides, front and neck, plus a cloth-covered, three-panel steel chamfron for the animal's head.

(**2b**) Schematic arrangement of the main elements of the horse armour and their constituent lames. The red box indicates the area shown in detail in 2c and 2d.

(**2c**) Exterior of the indicated upper corner of the chest armour showing the straps supporting the horizontal laminated leather lames.

(**2d**) Interior of the indicated upper corner of the chest armour showing a layer of quilted cloth to support this uppermost part of the horse armour.

(**3a–3c**) Decorated 15th-century steel chamfrons.

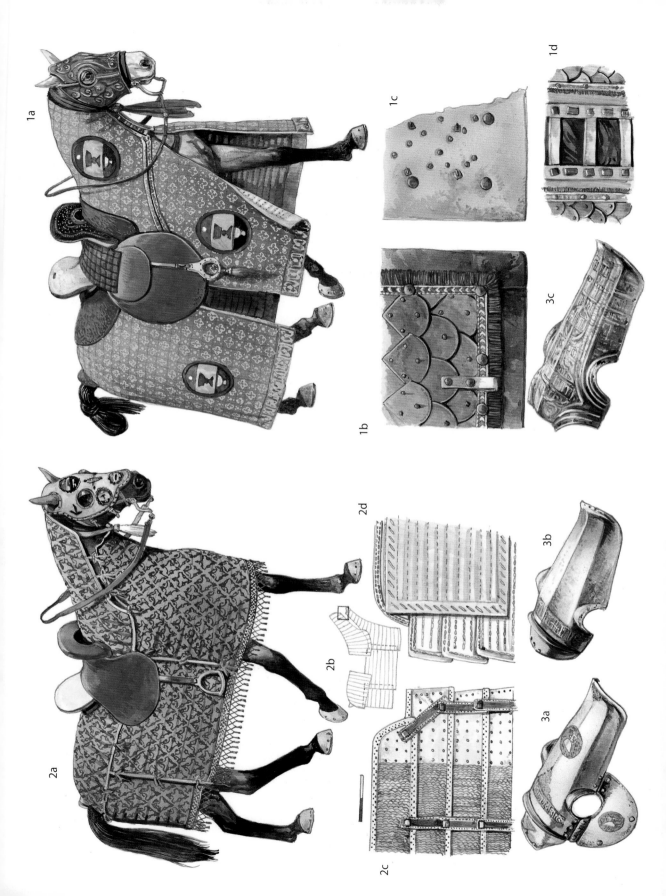

ر[Arabic text at top of illustration]

[Arabic text below illustration]

Kitab al-makhzun was a Mamluk collection of earlier *furusiyah* texts. The copy shown was made in Egypt in 1474 and illustrates cavalry in training, one wielding a mace and one a horse-archer shooting at a *qabaq* high target. (Ms. Or. C.686, Oriental Institute Library, Academy of Sciences, St Petersburg)

rulers stood in this league is unclear but they were almost always older, more experienced men. It should be noted that all *mamluks* were better trained than *halqa* troops. During the latter half of the 15th century written evidence suggests a decline in the length, and perhaps intensity, of military training, as well as a decline in obedience, loyalty, respect for elderly *mamluks* and promotion on merit. However, even in the final years of the Sultanate the majority of *mamluk* recruits still went through the military schools.

New recruits to the elite corps were educated in a *tabaq* (pl. *tabaqah*) barrack within the palace area of the Citadel of Cairo. Here, according to Ibn Khaldun, teachers were to: 'foster their loyalty and give them a careful upbringing including the study of the Koran and other subjects of instruction, until they become proficient in these things. Then they train them in the use of the bow and the sword, in riding, in the *maydans*, in fighting with the spear, until they become tough and seasoned soldiers.'

According to the chronicler al-Zahiri there were a dozen *tabaqah* in the Citadel, each probably taking recruits of the same linguistic origin, and when the youngsters paraded for their pay, recruits from four *tabaqah* appeared per day.

The teaching staff mostly consisted of eunuchs who are said to have imposed strict discipline, with no talking being allowed even during military exercises. Eunuchs had their own ranking structure like that of other *mamluks* and from the late 12th century onward some retired as free men to form a guard of about 40 men for the Tomb of the Prophet in Medina. Here, their leader had the rank of *amir* while most of his men were well-educated, devoted readers of the Koran and spoke many languages. They kept in touch with their previous masters in Egypt and perhaps also with other retired eunuch *mamluks* who guarded the tombs of departed sultans.[9]

The German knight Arnold von Harff claimed to have visited Egypt between 1496 and 1499 and in his account of his travels he admitted to being surprised by the way young *mamluks* trained in the Citadel:

> As one enters the first gate there is on the right hand a large building, in which are many large rooms, wherein the young mamluks have thirty-two masters, who teach them writing, reading, fighting with lances, also to defend themselves with the small shield, shooting with the hand-bow at a target, and all kinds of feats of skill. I saw five hundred young mamluks in this building all standing by a wall with outstretched arms as if about to climb the wall on hands and feet. I enquired why they behaved so foolishly, and was told that this was to make their arms and other limbs supple.[10]

9 de Angelis, V., *Eunuchi*, Casale Monferrato (2000) pp.266–270.
10 Von Harff, Arnold (tr. M. Letts), *The Pilgrimage of Arnold von Harff, Knight*, London (1946) p.106.

Although the religious education of the *mamluk* class may have left something to be desired, they were far from being uncultured. There was a strong interest in works of *adab*, or 'gentlemanly knowledge', in Muslim religious traditions with military associations, and in stories which offered examples of correct behaviour. *Mamluks* naturally had an interest in *furusiyah* military training manuals and a few wrote, compiled or annotated such texts.

Furusiyah had a broad meaning, encompassing military skill and individual character but was not the same as *shuja'a* courage. From at least the 9th century onwards *furusiyah al-harbiyah* or 'military *furusiyah*' focused primarily upon the training of *ghulam* or *mamluk* soldiers. However, this training was not confined to cavalry skills and included the use of all weapons, both on horseback and on foot, knowledge of armour, siege warfare, hunting and, eventually, naval warfare. Though the Mamluk Sultanate took the lead in compiling and writing later medieval works on *furusiyah*, these were largely based upon earlier texts, especially those of the mid-9th-century 'Abbasid commander Ibn Akhi Hizam, with some updating to include modern weapons.

The main branches of *furusiyah* remained *la'b al-rumh* and *thaqafat al-rumh* (use of the cavalry spear), *darb al-sayf* (swordplay), and *fann al-dabbus* (use of the mace). The main exercises in *al-nushshab*, or archery, were the *qabaq* shooting at a raised gourd and *sawq al-birjas* shooting at a low target, both from close range. Long-distance 'flight-shooting' was another important skill. However, the *qaws al-bunduq* pellet bow was used in hunting, while the crossbow was used in both hunting and siege or naval warfare. *Sira'* was wrestling while *sawq al-mahmil* were display 'games' associated with the *mahmal* procession during the *Hajj* pilgrimage. *La'b al-kura* and *la'b al-sawlajan* were polo while *sibaq al-khayl* was horse racing.

One of the most practical *furusiyah* manuscripts from the Mamluk era is the *Nihayat al-Su'l*, a mixture of old and new information compiled in the

The Mamluk elite sponsored a variety of religious buildings to demonstrate their piety and enhance their legitimacy. One of these was the Dar al-Kuran al-Karim al-Sabaniya in Damascus which dates from 1463–64. It was a Koranic teaching *madrasah* college. (Author's photograph)

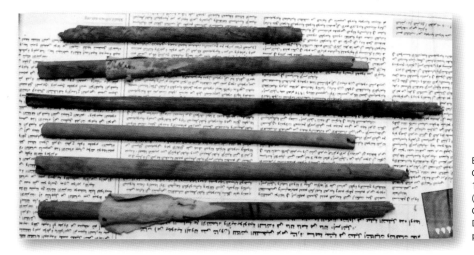

Broken crossbow bolts from the Citadel of Damascus from the 13th to the mid-14th centuries. (Syrian National Museum Conservation Department, Damascus; author's photograph)

late 13th to the early 14th centuries. It is often presented in a simple question-and-answer style, suitable for a soldier rather than a scholar or armchair general. The *Nihayat al-Su'l* is also unusual in providing detailed information about armour, putting it on and taking it off – sometimes in an emergency – its repair and its maintenance.

The evidence of *furusiyah* and other texts suggest that the mid-13th and early 14th centuries were a time when skill with the cavalry spear was rated above all other weapons, though this did not necessarily mean there was a decline in horse-archery. In fact the 'arts of the spear' were normally divided into four parts:

1 – Training in handling the weapon, types of charge and thrust, and spear combat when not actually charging;

2 – *Bunud* exercises consisting of set movements for a single horseman, manoeuvring his horse and parrying an opponent's thrusts;

3 – *Manasib* mock combats between two men, at least one of whom was armed with a spear;

4 – *Mayadin* simulated combat between two teams of horsemen.

The Mamluk Sultanate did not produce new works on archery until the second half of the 14th and the 15th centuries, having previously relied upon earlier 'Abbasid works. Even the famous mid-14th-century book on archery by Ibn Mangli relied upon a monumental 13th-century text by a Moroccan

ARMS AND ARMOUR OF THE 15TH AND EARLY 16TH CENTURIES

(**1**) Middle ranking *amir* of the late 15th or very early 16th century, wearing a partially gilded helmet with a sliding nasal, a mail-lined *kazaghand* and a scale-lined *qarqal*. The separate flap-like upper arm protections of the *qarqal* are based upon pictorial, rather than archaeological, evidence. He is armed with a sabre, a dagger and full archery equipment.

(**2a**) Late 15th century *qarqal* covered in striped velvet and lined with steel scales on two layers of linen canvas. The additional horizontal webbing straps at the shoulders would be used to secure arm defences, which are not shown because they no longer existed on the *qarqal* found in the Citadel of Damascus, upon which this reconstruction is based.

(**2b**) Small, linked steel plates that probably protected the shoulders.

(**2c**) Copper buckle used to close the front of the *qarqal*.

(**3**) Mail and plate cuirass of the most decorated type, dating from the late 15th century. The uppermost rows of mail links forming the neck of this armour are horizontally laced with rawhide thongs to make the collar semi-stiff. The main body of the cuirass consists of a mail hauberk with large, flattened links, plus gilded steel horizontal lames.

(**4**) Mail and plate armour for the thigh and knee.

(**5a**) Decorated helmet with cheek and neck pieces, plus a sliding nasal.

(**5b**) Undecorated helmet with cheek and neck pieces, plus a sliding nasal.

(**5c**) Helmet with a neck guard and sliding nasal.

(**5d**) Helmet with engraved decoration, cheek pieces and sliding nasal.

(**5e**) Fluted helmet with engraved decoration around the brow-band.

(**6a**) Exterior of an engraved steel shield.

(**6b**) Interior of the steel shield.

(**7**) Sabre.

(**8a**) Dagger with a bronze pommel, leather-covered wooden grip, and bronze quillons.

(**8b and 8c**) Both sides of a leather-covered wooden sheath with a bronze chape covered in kid leather.

(**9a**) Decorated war axe with a half-moon blade.

(**9b**) War axe with a 'bearded' blade and a *mamluk* heraldic blazon.

(**9c**) Small-headed war axe with gilded decoration.

(**10**) Steel lance head with a plain blade and a decorated socket.

(**11**) Engraved steel standard in the shape of a broad spearhead.

5a 5b 5c 5d 5e

1 4

6a 11 10

6b 3

7 8a 2b

2c

8b 8c

9a 9b 9c 2a

named Ibn Maymun. The first truly original Mamluk work was by Taybugha al-Baklamishi, who focused upon horse-archery and the use of the composite 'Damascus bow'. This bow was made in a limited number of sizes and strengths and could, therefore, be produced in an almost modern production-line system. The main 15th-century Mamluk treatise on archery was probably that by Muhammad Ibn 'Ali al-Sughayyir, but it was written for experts rather than beginners.

The *Munyatu'l-Guzat* was a 14th-century Mamluk-Kipchaq Turkish version of an Arabic original. Its description of archery training was highly specific and included details of close-range shooting at a wicker basket filled with sand:

> When you wish to start shooting arrows on horseback [while] riding, you should take a weak bow and arrow … Then erect five targets that are following each other. The distance between each of them should be forty cubits. Then take five arrows, ride your horse fast and shoot these one after the other. When you become good at shooting at these, make the distance between them thirty cubits. Every time reduce like that, until the distance is seven paces. When you also become skilful at this, try to shoot fast.[11]

Archery training at a high target was intended to improve a shooter's dexterity, while shooting to the rear was more of a 'party trick'.

Long-range or flight-shooting was another exercise that developed strength and skill. In contrast, shower shooting was a real military skill that focused upon grouping several arrows within a limited target area. It required constant practice for the archer to become fast and accurate, so there was a special *maydan* or open training area in Cairo for such flight-shooting.

The *Nihayat al-Su'l* offered advice about a variety of weapons including the lasso used by Turks and Mongols – the author laid particular stress on how to avoid getting caught by a lasso. Instruction on the use of a sword was more extensive although it seemed more concerned with infantry

11 Öztopçu, K. (tr.), Munyatu'u-Ghuzāt, *A 14th Century Mamluk-Kipchak Military Treatise* (Sources of Oriental Languages and Literatures 13, Turkish Sources XI), Cambridge, Mass. (1989) p.77.

rather than cavalry warfare. A section on how to cross the Euphrates emphasized the importance of a soldier being able to swim: 'Above all he must practice throughout his life, and make a habit of swimming and being used to water, to understand its nature and how to keep himself [alive] in it.'

Maintaining the *maydan* training grounds was essential for training and a failure to do so was regarded as negligence. Some sultans were, of course, more enthusiastic than others. Baybars I reportedly went to the *maydan* every day from noon until the evening prayer, but to avoid overcrowding, only two from every ten *amirs* or *mamluks* were allowed to accompany him. There were

The *Khanaqah* dervish convent and Mausoleum of Sultan Barquq in medieval Cairo's northern cemetery still has some of its stained glass windows. Famines and political turbulence delayed the building's construction and it was not completed until 1412. (Author's photograph)

several specialized *maydans* around Cairo; the Maydan al-Salihi next to the Nile was for polo and dated from the late Ayyubid period but was abandoned when the river Nile shifted its bed westward. The Maydan al-Sibaq on the other side of the Citadel was built during the rule of Sultan Baybars and was probably for flight-shooting.

The Maydan Birkit al-Fil 'Maydan of the Elephant's Pool', built by Kitbugha in 1294–96, overlooked a seasonal pond but became a fashionable residential area after 1317. Some of these *maydans* were pleasant spots with stables, wells, water wheels, public drinking places and palms or other trees. Others had private kiosks for the sultan and his *amirs*.

Given their structured and intensive training it is hardly surprising that professional *mamluk* armies developed tactics to avoid the once-feared Crusader cavalry charges. Their greater mobility, superior discipline and probably more advanced battlefield communications enabled the *mamluks* to envelop the enemy, attacking from the flanks and rear. *Mamluk* speed of reaction also enabled units to retreat out of range when their officers saw Crusader crossbowmen preparing to raise and shoot their weapons.

It is perhaps true that Mamluk commanders continued the old tradition of putting Arab Bedouin cavalry on one wing and Turkomans on the other, while keeping their strongest forces in the centre. However, such information comes from *furusiyah* treatises

A page from the late 15th-century Mamluk *Kitab al-makhzun* showing a cavalryman displaying his riding skills in the *maydan*, or hippodrome. (Ms. Or. C.686, Oriental Institute Library, Academy of Sciences, St Petersburg)

These pellets of unfired clay from the Citadel of Damascus, which would be shot from a *qaws bunduq* pellet bow, are probably Mamluk. (IFPO; Patrick Godeau's photograph).

which tended to be unoriginal in their tactical advice. These texts were mostly collections of works by respected earlier writers, relevant or otherwise, including those by Ancient and Byzantine Greeks, Sassanian Iranians and earlier Muslim 'Abbasid theorists. On the other hand, the author of the *Nihayat al-Su'l* tried to update his quotations from the 2nd-century Greco-Roman military scholar Aelianus Tacticus, one example being his description of how to lay an ambush:

The ambush site should preferably be scouted for by choosing a position close to water so that, should the operation be delayed, they will not be afflicted by thirst ... The track to water should be level so that horses do not jostle upon it. The site of the ambush should be in a place where there is no fear of a snatch raid against the look-out post by night or day, in a dominant situation so that anyone who shows himself is clearly visible ... They should abandon rash or confused action wherever they are but should rather be quiet and maintain silence, and should not startle wild animals or birds... Equally, the roving scouts should keep a close and unremitting watch on the enemy situation... Once they have gained their objective they should return straight to their positions, not leaving any one of them behind. If one man's horse is lame, one of the group should seat him behind himself on his mount; they should not abandon him for in so doing there considerable harm to morale... Once the members of the ambush group have been designated, the commander of the force should divide them into three groups. One of them should go to a position not farther than 2,000 paces from one side of the two flanks of the vanguard forces, being in a position close to the open flank of the enemy, as close as the Unbelievers' battle line will allow ... If the force should become enfeebled, the ambush party at the rear will be a

G

MAMLUK CAVALRY TRAINING, MID-14TH CENTURY

Two pairs of men are involved in different forms of *furusiyah* military training at the southern end of the Great Maydan, outside the Citadel of Cairo. Figures (1) and (2) undertake a spear exercise while (3) and (4) undertake a mace exercise using short bamboo staves.

The inset 'plans' show cavalry formation manoeuvres in *furusiyah* manuscripts dating from the Mamluk period.

(5) 'The Tenth *maydan*, the two hooks are divided, turned, they play the Frank [European]', in a Mamluk copy of *Nihayat al-Su'l* made in 1371. (British Library, Add. Ms. 18866, f.93r, London)

(6) 'The joining of two opposing teams in the *maydan* before a large public', from *Umdat al-mujahidin fi tartib al-mayadin* [Movements of combatants concerning the arrangement of carousels]' by Husam al-Din al-Rammah (died 1337), Mamluk copy made in 1395. (Bibliothèque National, Ms. Arabe 6604, f.4v, Paris)

(7) 'The arrangements of parades', from one of the scattered pages of a copy of al-Tabari's *Kitab majmu' fi'l-rumh wa ghayrihi* made in 1466. (Keir Collection, no.II.8, London)

reinforcement for them … Now that is what happened in the year 702 AH [AD 1303] at the battle of Marj al-Saffar [when a Mamluk army decisively defeated a Mongol Il-Khanid invasion of Syria].[12]

With such a wealth of knowledge and experience, it is no surprise that *mamluk* deserters were welcomed by less advanced neighbours. For example, early in the 15th century an ex-*mamluk* of the governor of Damascus, named Altunbugha, became governor of Qus in upper Egypt. He then abandoned his post and offered his services to the Negus Yeshaq I of Ethiopia, offering to train his troops in the use of lance, archery, sabre and siege machines. Around the same time some Circassian *mamluk* deserters led by a presumed officer named al-Tabingha also arrived in Ethiopia, amongst them an armourer who established an arsenal to make weapons and mail. He also taught the Ethiopians to use *naft* or 'Greek Fire' incendiaries. Negus Yeshaq I is similarly said to have adopted sumptuous costume and a green turban in imitation of Mamluk fashions.[13]

EXPERIENCE OF BATTLE

Ibn Khaldun, the famous historian and philosopher who spent much of his working life in Mamluk Egypt, saw war as a distinctly human phenomenon, unseen elsewhere in God's Creation. He also interpreted war as a logical outcome of the concept of sovereignty and of the need to maintain sovereignty by force of arms.

For the armies of the Mamluk Sultanate, and especially the *mamluk* elite resident in Cairo, the geography of Egypt had a profound impact upon their experience of campaigning. The most important part of the army was based in Cairo but its most important campaigns were against Crusader States and Mongol invaders in greater Syria. Hence the *mamluks* had considerable experience of taking the desert road across northern Sinai, a march that necessitated the carrying or pre-positioning of fodder for large numbers of animals. Once the army reached more fertile territory in Palestine and Syria it probably relied upon local markets for fodder, though this again entailed forward planning by an efficient military bureaucracy.

Like a modern army, the Mamluk army had a substantial 'tail', much of it clearly non-combatant. The *mamluks* were also modern in that they rarely lived off the land – hence the need for properly defended supply trains as well as huge numbers of baggage animals. According to Emanuele Piloti, an early 15th-century Venetian from Crete, when on the march through friendly territory the Mamluk army normally sent its transport a day ahead of the main body of the army, protected by a vanguard of 2,000 cavalry. Perhaps the transport also carried food supplies. The centre of the line of march also had 2,000 cavalry, while the sultan personally commanded the rearguard. On major campaigns, 13th- and 14th-century *mamluks* each received one or two baggage camels whereas every two non-elite *halqa* soldiers shared three camels. However, daily marches that proved longer or more difficult than

12 Tantum, G., 'Muslim Warfare: A Study of a Medieval Muslim Treatise on the Art of ar', in Elgood, R. (ed.), *Islamic Arms and Armour*, London (1979) pp.198–20.
13 Wiet, G., 'Les relations Égypto-abyssines sous les sultans Mamlouks', *Bulletin de la Société d'archéologie copte*, 4 (1938) p.120.

The Citadel of Cairo was the Mamluk Sultanate's main training centre and was soon almost surrounded by large religious buildings sponsored by Mamluk rulers or senior military leaders. These included the mosque and *khanaqah* or dervish convent of Shaykh Nizam al-Din Ishaq, built in 1356. (Author's photograph)

expected could cause strain and weaken logistical support while undermining morale and causing friction within the command structure. Such problems were even worse if a pitched battle dragged on longer than planned.

A concern for morale and a tradition of efficient administration lay behind the cleanliness and good order of *mamluk* military camps, especially during sieges such as that of Acre in 1291. Such encampments had baths with warm water and professional attendants, along with latrines for the officers and probably for ordinary *mamluks*. In fact, during one Crusader sortie from besieged Acre, an enemy knight fell into an *amir*'s latrine and was killed.

Of course, warfare against the Crusaders was not confined to Palestine and Syria. Egypt was targeted by land and sea, culminating in the battle of Mansura in 1250 when senior *mamluk amirs* also initiated their takeover of the Ayyubid state. Another 'front' against the Crusader States was in mountainous northern Lebanon where the *mamluks* called upon specialist 'mountain troops' of Turkish origin when attacking the cave-fortress, or refuge grotto, of Asi'l-Hadath. Here, recent archaeological excavations have produced a remarkable array of clothing and weaponry dating from 1283 when Asi'l-Hadath was finally overrun. Interestingly enough, comparable specialist Turkish 'mountain troops' were employed by the Mongols in Iran.

As in medieval European warfare, the losses suffered by a victorious army were often remarkably low. At the successful siege of Acre in 1291, for example, only seven *amirs* and 30 *amirs' mamluks*, six commanders of the *halqa* and 53 *halqa* troops were killed, though the numbers of volunteers who lost their lives is not recorded. Also during the siege of Acre, the severed heads of slain Crusaders were paraded, hung from the saddles of captured horses. Whether this was done by *mamluks* or tribal troops is unknown. Of course, the Muslims were not always victorious and captured *mamluks* could endure prolonged periods as enslaved prisoners of war. Strenuous efforts were made to get such men released, though the Mamluk government also liked to use such releases for propaganda purposes. They, therefore, preferred to use the funds of an Islamic charitable *waqf*, established in Damascus for this specific purpose, rather than pay humiliating ransoms. Even when

The Mamluks are credited with writing many books on *furusiyah*, though these manuscripts were mostly copies of earlier 9th- or 10th-century works. However, some illustrations from the period incorporate modern weapons such as the archaic handheld gun shown on a page made around 1460. (Keir Collection, London)

Several Mamluk religious buildings preserve features that would also have been seen in Mamluk palaces. An example is this elaborate painted ceiling in the Mosque of Barsbay, dating from 1437, in the Nile Delta town of Khanqah. (Author's photograph)

treaties with the Crusaders allowed the release of prisoners, a treaty presupposed peace and recognition of the enemy, which the sultanate was politically loathe to do.

Campaigns against the Mongols could be very different, yet the elite cavalry of both sides may have had more in common than is generally realized. Recent Russian studies suggest that fully armoured, close-combat cavalry formed an increasingly important part of Mongol and Il-Khanid armies. Clearly, the army that the *mamluks* faced at 'Ayn Jalut in 1260 was no tribal horde. The resulting battle has sometimes been described as an ambush, but in reality it was a classic example of Mamluk tactics, drawing their enemy into unfavourable terrain and into a trap. 'Ayn Jalut also demonstrated how infantry could still play a major role, especially in hilly country. Other *mamluk* cavalry units conducted the battle in a traditional manner, with repeated attacks and withdrawals by units whose movements were controlled by flags and drums, until the Mongols collapsed.

Over the following decades *mamluk* success or failure against the Il-Khanids often reflected political conditions within the sultanate. These had a strong impact upon the leadership of field armies, especially if political changes led to the dismissal or disgrace of senior *amirs* and the downgrading of their *mamluk* units. With rivals on almost every side, the Mamluk Sultanate sent its troops against a remarkable array of different enemies. Occasionally, *mamluks* also had to fight internal foes, as when Baybars finally crushed the power of the Arab Bedouin in Upper Egypt.

It seems that the Muslim authorities in Aswan traditionally expected the northern Nubian kingdom of Nobatia to keep the neighbouring and troublesome Beja nomads in check. In practice direct Nubian control rarely extended much beyond the Nile valley and there was a steep decline in Nubian power from the mid-13th century onwards. By the 1260s the northern Nubian states of Nobatia and Makuria were almost encircled by Muslim tribes. Around the time of the first Mamluk invasion of northern Nubia in 1265, the *mamluks* were also completing their conquest of the Red Sea coastal region of Suakin and the Dahlak Islands. Meanwhile, the Mamluk Sultanate extended its domination over the oases of Egypt's Western Desert, north-eastern Libya and the Hijaz in Arabia.

Aggression was not always one-sided and in 1381 Ethiopian raiders attacked what was by then largely Islamized Nubia. Not content with raiding territory under Mamluk suzerainty, this Ethiopian force pressed on to reach Aswan in Egypt itself. It was said to have been commanded by Dawit, a future *Negus*, or king, of Ethiopia. He probably chose that moment to attack

Leather quiver for arrows, probably 15th-century Mamluk. (Museum of Islamic Art, Cairo; author's photograph)

knowing of the current confusion in Egypt where the largely Turkish Bahri sultans were giving way to the largely Circassian Burji sultans.

Within a few years, the Mamluk state would be plunged into another life-or-death struggle, this time against Timur-i Lang, who posed a threat as mortal as that previously posed by the Mongols. The sultanate survived and even seemed to flourish but then came a catastrophic defeat in 1481, at the hands of a seemingly minor foe, the Dulghadir Turkoman rulers of south-eastern Anatolia. Having previously enjoyed a number of successes, the *mamluks* faced the loss of many senior and experienced *amirs*, as well as a substantial number of trained men. This setback was made worse by the increasing difficulty of recruiting new *mamluks* and paying those already serving.

However, there do not seem to have been significant problems with *mamluk* morale. The presence of *sufi* dervishes on the battlefield praying for victory, or even praying from afar, was seen as a good omen. Even so, commanders took more practical steps, as at the battle of Marj al-Suffar in 1302 when 'grooms' were stationed behind the main army to stop any *mamluks* who tried to flee.

The *mamluks'* dislike of being stationed on the coast or, even worse, being sent on a naval campaign is well known. Such postings lacked prestige and could be very dangerous. Even during minor incidents such as the Genoese raids on Sidon in 1383, the defenders of coastal fortifications suffered heavily, in this case at the hands of Genoese crossbowmen. On the other hand, the idea that the Mamluk Sultanate had no interest in naval warfare is simply untrue. Shipbuilding may have slumped and fleets may have been constructed only when needed, but there were clearly enough crews to man the fleets which transported *mamluk* armies to Cyprus, Rhodes and on campaigns in the Red Sea.

Whereas *mamluk* forces achieved notable successes in Cyprus during the mid-15th century, a longer-distance assault upon the centre of Hospitaller power in Rhodes was convincingly defeated. This ambitious campaign was not undertaken on a whim or out of inflated ambition; rather Hospitaller Rhodes was regarded a major threat to Mamluk trade and communications. Therefore, following Sultan Barsbay's triumph against the

In this Mamluk copy of the Persian *Shahnamah* verse-epic, which was made around 1510, assorted combat techniques and a mounted trumpeter appear in a battle between Persians and Turks. (Topkapi Lib. Ms. Haz.1519, f.160a, Istanbul)

The Mamluk period was the golden age of Cairo's surviving architecture and among the most typical of the 'courtyard style' later medieval mosques is that of Altinbugha al-Maridani, the *saqi* cup-bearer and son-in-law of Sultan al-Nasir Muhammad. It was built between 1339 and 1341. (Author's photograph)

Fragments of two sewn leather containers, which may have been quivers or bow cases, from the Citadel of Damascus – 15th to early 16th centuries. (IFPO; Patrick Godeau's photograph)

Kingdom of Cyprus, his successor Sultan Jaqmaq swore to destroy the Hospitaller 'nest of pirates'.

The fleet that Jaqmaq sent in 1440 consisted of 15 ships and about 1,000 troops but, after some skirmishing, achieved nothing. Jaqmaq realized that he needed a larger fleet. This set out in 1443 and initially enjoyed success against the outlying Hospitaller island of Kastellorizo before being forced home by deteriorating weather. The third expedition left in 1444. A significant naval clash off the coast of Rhodes ended with equal honours, which was remarkable enough considering the Mamluks' poor reputation in naval warfare and the very different reputation of the Hospitallers. Thereupon, the Mamluk army came ashore but was defeated while in its own supposed element, fighting a land battle, and so sailed home.

The idea that the *mamluks* were reluctant to adopt new gunpowder weapons is as inaccurate as their supposed unwillingness to engage in naval warfare. In fact, the Mamluk Sultanate probably adopted the idea of ox-drawn carts containing handgunners and a single light bronze cannon from the Ottoman Turks, eventually having about 100 such battle waggons. In the last battle of all at Raydaniya, north-east of Cairo, the *mamluks* placed their cannon behind field fortifications consisting of a trench backed by an embankment upon which the guns were placed. In the event, of course, it was the *mamluks* rather than the Ottomans who suffered appalling losses from modern firearms with few of the elite troops apparently falling to traditional weapon.

Large number of *mamluks* were killed by the Ottoman Sultan Selim the Grim during and after his conquest of Egypt, though the proportion of those slain to those who survived is unknown. Clearly, the upper ranks of *amirs* were almost totally wiped out, but many ordinary *mamluks* initially escaped or merged into the wider population. The Ottomans did not target the *awlad al-nas*, sons of *mamluks*, though many families had to pay hefty ransoms. Those who feared being identified as *mamluks* also abandoned distinctive *mamluk* costume such as the *zamt* fluffy red hat and the *takhfifa* method of winding a turban. Instead, they adopted the headgear of those humbler members of society from whom the *mamluks* had previously been at pains to separate themselves.

H

THE BATTLE OF KHIROKITIA (7 JULY 1426)

The Mamluk expeditionary force that invaded Cyprus crushed the army of the Lusignan Crusader Kingdom of Cyprus at the battle of Khirokitia, despite having recently brought its cavalry horses on a substantial sea-crossing. In fact, proper *mamluks*, here represented by an *amir* officer (**1**), a standard bearer (**2**) and a middle ranking *'askari* (**3**), formed only a small élite within the invading force. Most of the army consisted of second-line troops (**4**) plus large numbers of Arab, and other, irregulars. Initially, the outnumbered *'askaris* feared that they would be overwhelmed, but they are said to have been urged to fight for Islam and to fight because there would be no hope of escape if they were defeated. The *mamluk* charge then smashed through the Cypriot line (**5** to **7**) and captured King Janus of Cyprus (**8**).

The harsh anti-*mamluk* measures that had followed the Ottoman conquest eased after 1517, especially after Selim the Grim returned to Istanbul. A short while later, surviving *mamluks* were again allowed to ride horses and purchase weapons. Thereafter, they and their descendants were gradually absorbed into the Ottoman military structure in Egypt and eventually came to dominate it again during the 18th century.

COLLECTIONS AND SIGNIFICANT HISTORICAL LOCATIONS

The most famous Mamluk structures in Cairo are either of stone or are faced with stone. However, some buildings in smaller towns in Egypt show the skills of Mamluk-period architects using brick and stucco. This photograph shows an example of a *muqarnas* decoration on the early 14th-century Mosque of al-Ma'ini in Dumyat. (Author's photograph)

Most surviving Mamluk military equipment, apart from recent archaeological discoveries, had been reused by the Ottoman Turks. Such reuse was characteristic of the Ottomans, especially where arms and armour taken from their Muslim rivals were concerned. A certain amount of this war material was then captured again by the Ottoman Empire's European foes. Despite this, the largest single collection of Mamluk military equipment is to be found in Istanbul, mostly in the Topkapi Museum, though to a lesser and more debateable degree in the Askeri (Army) Museum. The bulk of this had been stored for centuries in the St Irene Church within the grounds of the Topkapi Palace which served as a sort of armoury of military relics and trophies. During the 19th century, however, many of the finest Ottoman and Mamluk pieces in this 'St Irene Collection', with their characteristic simplified *tugra* mark, were sold – legally or otherwise – to collectors from around the world.

Some of the sacred religious relics, such as swords correctly or incorrectly associated with the Prophet Muhammad, his successors and other heroes of early Islam, had been given replacement hilts when they formed part of a religious reliquary within the Mamluk Sultanate. These relics were also taken to Istanbul by the victorious Ottomans and are now divided between the Topkapi Palace, the Topkapi Museum and the Askeri Museum.

Most of the pieces that were sold during the 19th century initially went into private collections. From there the best bits, including Mamluk armour and weapons, were subsequently acquired by museums in Europe, Russia and the USA. The most significant objects are probably now those in the Hermitage Museum in St Petersburg, the Royal Armouries in Leeds (England), the Louvre in Paris, the Musée Royale d'Art et d'Histoire in Brussels, the Museo Nazionale di Bargello in Florence and the Metropolitan Museum of Art in New York.

Surprisingly few correctly identified pieces of Mamluk military equipment can be seen in Egyptian and Syrian museums. Furthermore,

In another scene from the late Mamluk-era copy of the *Shahnamah* made for Sultan Qansawh II al-Ghawri, Rustam grieves after slaying his son Suhrab. (Topkapi Lib. Ms. Haz.1519, f.160a, Istanbul)

most of the abundant Mamluk military artefacts and elements of clothing that have been found recently in Syria, and to a lesser extent in Egypt, have yet to be put on display in museums. Descriptions of many of them have yet to be published and a great number still need to be cleaned and conserved. How much of such material found in Syria that still awaits study, conservation and display, will survive the current civil war is a matter that gives the author many sleepless nights!

In Syria several important sites have already been damaged. However, in Egypt the situation is better where locations associated with the Mamluk Sultanate are concerned. Most Mamluk military architecture consisted of strengthenings, additions and extensions to existing fortifications. In Egypt the Citadel of Cairo was the most important single location for the Mamluks, but most of its walls and towers were built by the preceding Ayyubid sultans. Most of what the Mamluks added within the Citadel has been lost, with the notable exception of the early Mamluk Mosque of al-Nasir. Elsewhere, in what was later medieval Cairo, there are an astonishing number of buildings dating from the Mamluk era, though most are religious rather than domestic or military. The same is true of several other parts of the country, to the extent that the Mamluks are better remembered as builders than as soldiers.

Essentially, the same can be said of the great cities of Syria, especially Damascus. Within the coastal regions of Syria, however, most Mamluk fortifications were added to existing Crusader rather than earlier Islamic military architecture. Indeed, with only a few dramatic exceptions, most of what are described as 'Crusader castles' are, in reality, largely of Mamluk date. This is also true of Jordan, Lebanon, Israel and Palestine. There are further significant Mamluk fortifications and some interesting non-military architecture in southern Turkey, though here the Mamluks largely took over and strengthened Armenian castles.

FURTHER READING

Allan, J. W., 'Mamlūk Sultanic Heraldry and the Numismatic Evidence: A Reinterpretation', *Journal of the Royal Asiatic Society* (1970) pp.99–112

Amitai, R., 'The Logistics of the Mongol–Mamlūk War, with Special Reference to the Battle of Wādī'l-Khaznadār, 1299 C.E.', in Pryor, J. H. (ed.), *Logistics of Warfare in the Age of the Crusades*, Aldershot (2006) pp.25–42

Amitai, R., 'Mamlūk Espionage among Mongols and Franks', *Asian and African Studies*, 22 (1988) pp.173–181

Amitai, R., 'The Mamluk Officer Class during the Reign of Sultan Baybars', in Lev, Y. (ed.), *War and Society in the Eastern Mediterranean, 7th–15th Centuries*, Leiden (1996) pp.267–300

Amitai, R., *Mongols and Mamluks: The Mamluk–Ikhanid War, 1260–1281*, Cambridge (1995)

Amitai, R., 'The Remaking of the Military Elite of Mamluk Egypt by al-Nāsir Muhammad b. Qalāwūn', *Studia Islamica*, 72 (1990) pp.145–163

Anon. (ed.), *The Mamluks and the Early Ottoman Period in Bilad al-Sham: History and Archaeology. ARAM 9-10*, Oxford (1997–98)

Ansarī, 'Umar ibn Ibrahim al-Awsī al- (ed. & tr. Scanlon, G. T.), *A Muslim Manual of War: Being Tafrīj al-Kurūb fī Tadbīr al-Hurūb*, Cairo (1961 & 2012)

Ashtor, E., *Histoire des Prix et des salaires dans l'orient médiéval*, Paris (1969)

Ashtor, E., & Kedar, B. Z., 'Una Guerra fra Genova e i Mamlucchi negli anni 1380', *Archivio Storico Italiano*, 133 (1975) pp.3–44

Atasoy, N., '1510 Tarihli Memlûk Şehnamesinin Minyatürleri', *Sanat Tarihi Yilligi* (1968) pp.48–69

Ayalon, D., 'Aspects of the Mamlūk Phenomenon: B. Ayyubids, Kurds and Turks', *Der Islam*, 54 (1977) pp.1–32

Ayalon, D., 'Aspects of the Mamlūk Phenomenon: The Importance of the Mamlūk Institution', *Der Islam*, 53 (1976) pp.196–225

Ayalon, D., 'The Circassians in the Mamluk Kingdom', *Journal of the American Oriental Society*, 69 (1949) pp.135–147

Ayalon, D., 'Discharges from Service, Banishments and Imprisonments in Mamluk Society', *Israel Oriental Studies*, 2 (1972) pp.25–50

Ayalon, D., 'Eunuchs in the Mamlūk Sultanate', in Rosen-Ayalon, M. (ed.), *Studies in Memory of Gaston Wiet*, Jerusalem (1977) pp.267–295

Ayalon, D., *Gunpowder and Firearms in the Mamluk Kingdom*, London (1956)

Ayalon, D., 'Mamlūk Military Aristocracy during the First Years of the Ottoman Occupation in Egypt', in Bosworth, C. E. (ed.), *The Islamic World from Classical to Modern Times: Essays in Honour of Bernard Lewis*, Princeton (1989) pp.413–431

Ayalon, D., 'Mamlūkiyyāt: (A) A First Attempt to Evaluate the Mamlūk Military System', '(B) Ibn Khaldūn's View of the Mamlūk Phenomenon', *Jerusalem Studies in Arabic and Islam*, 2 (1980) pp.321–349

Ayalon, D., 'The Muslim City and the Mamluk Military Aristocracy', *Proceedings of the Israel Academy of Sciences and Humanities*, 2 (1968) pp.311–329

Ayalon, D., 'Plague and Its Effect on the Mamluk Army', *Journal of the Royal Asiatic Society* (1946) pp.67–73

Ayalon, D., 'Le Régiment Bahriyya dans l'armée Mamelouke', *Revue des Études Islamiques* (1951) pp.133–141

Ayalon, D., 'Studies in the Structure of the Mamlūk Army I: The Army Stationed in Egypt', *Bulletin of the School of Oriental and African Studies*, 15 (1953) pp.203–228

Ayalon, D., 'Studies in the Structure of the Mamlūk Army III: Holders of Offices Connected with the Army', *Bulletin of the School of Oriental and African Studies*, 16 (1954) pp.57–90

Ayalon, D., 'The System of Payment in Mamluk Military Society', *Journal of the Economic and Social History of the Orient*, 1 (1958) pp.37–65 & 257–296

Behrens-Abouseif, D., 'The Citadel of Cairo: Stage for Mamluk Ceremonial', *Annales Islamologiques*, 24 (1988) pp.25–79

Brett, M., 'The Origins of the Mamluk Military System in the Fatimid Period', in Vermeulen, U. & Smet, D. De (eds), *Egypt and Syria in the Fatimid, Ayyubid and Mamluk Eras I*, Leuven (1995) pp.39–52

Christie, N., 'Reconstructing Life in Medieval Alexandria from an Eighth/Fourteenth Century *Waqf* Document', *Mamlūk Studies Review*, 8 (2004) pp.163–189

Christie, N., 'A Rental Document from 8th/14th century Egypt', *Journal of the American Research Center in Egypt*, 41 (2004) pp.161–172

De Giosa, S. L., 'Cairene Style in Jerusalem: Architectural Patronage in the Reign of Sultan Qaytbay', *Bulletin of the Council for British Research in the Levant*, 8 (2013) pp.52–54

Drory, J., 'Jerusalem during the Mamluk Period (1250–1517)', in Levine, L. I. (ed.), *The Jerusalem Cathedra: Studies in the History, Archaeology, Geography and Ethnography of the Land of Israel, vol. 1*, Jerusalem (1981) pp.190–213

Ehrenkreutz, A., 'Strategic Implications of the Slave Trade between Genoa and Mamluk Egypt in the Second Half of the Thirteenth Century', in Udovitch, A. L. (ed.), *The Islamic Middle East, 700–1900: Studies in Economic and Social History*, Princeton (1981) pp.335–345

Fons, E., 'Á propos des Mongols: Une lettre d'Ibn Taymiyya á sultan al-Malik al-Nāsir Muhammad b. Qalāwūn', *Annales islamologiques*, 43 (2009) pp.31–72

Forand, P. G., 'The Relation of the Slave and the Client to the Master or Patron in Medieval Islam', *International Journal of Middle Eastern Studies*, 2 (1971) pp.59–66

Fuess, A., 'Rotting Ships and Razed Harbours: The Naval Policy of the Mamluks', *Mamluk Studies Review*, 5 (2001) pp.45–71

Fuess, A., 'Sultans with Horns: The Political Significance of Headgear in the Mamluk Empire', *Mamluk Studies Review*, 12 (2008) pp.71–94

Gaudefroy Demombynes, M., *Syrie á l'Epoque Mameloukes d'aprés les Auteurs Arabes*, Paris (1923)

Gazda, D., 'Mameluke Invasions on Nubia in the 13th Century: Some Thoughts on Political Interrelations in the Middle East', *Gdansk Archaeological Museum Africa Reports*, 3 (2005) pp.93–98

Gonnella, J., 'Die aiyubidische und mamlukische Zitadelle von Aleppo: Residenzstadt und Befestigung', in Piana, M. (ed.), *Burgen und Städt der Kreuzzugzeit*, Petersberg (2008) pp.139–147

Haldane, D., 'Scenes of Daily Life from Mamluk Miniatures', in Holt, P. M. (ed.), *The Eastern Mediterranean Lands in the Period of the Crusades*, Warminster (1977) pp.78–89

Holt, P. M., *Early Mamluk Diplomacy (1260–1290)*, Leiden (1995)

Holt, P. M., 'The Sultan as Ideal Ruler: Ayyubid and Mamluk Prototypes', in M.

Kunt & Woodhead, C. (eds.), *Süleyman the Magnificent and His Age: The Ottoman Empire in the Early Modern World*, London (1995) pp.122–137

Horii, Y., 'The Mamlūk Sultan Qānsūh Qānsh al-Ghawri (1501–16) and the Venetians of Alexandria', *Orient: Report of the Society for Near Eastern Studies in Japan*, 38 (2003) pp.178–199

Humphreys, R. S., 'Ayyubids, Mamluks and the Latin East in the Thirteenth Century', *Mamluk Studies Review*, 2 (1998) pp.2–17

Humphreys, R. S., 'The Emergence of the Mamluk Army', *Studia Islamica*, 45 (1977) pp.67–99 & 147–182

Ibn as-Suqāʿī (ed. & tr. Sublet, J.), *Tālī Kitāb Wafayāt al-Aʿyān: Un fonctionairre chretien dans l'administration mamelouke*, Damascus (1974)

Ibn Iyās (ed. & tr. Wiet, G.), *Journal d'un Bourgeois du Caire*, Paris (1955)

Ibn Manglī (tr. Viré, F.), *Ibn Manglī, De la Chasse, Commerce des grands de ce monde avec les bêtes sauvages des deserts sans onde*, Paris (1984)

Irwin, R., "Alī al-Baghdādī and the Joy of Mamlūk Sex', in Kennedy, H. (ed.), *The Historiography of Islamic Egypt (c.950–1800)*, Leiden (2001) pp.45–57

Irwin, R., 'Factions in Medieval Egypt', *Journal of the Royal Asiatic Society* (1986) pp.228–246

Irwin, R., 'Gunpowder and Firearms in the Mamluk Sultanate Reconsidered', in Winter, M. & Levanoni, A. (eds.), *The Mamluks in Egyptian and Syrian Politics and Society*, Leiden (2003) pp.117–139

Irwin, R., *The Middle East in the Middle Ages: The Early Mamluk Sultanate 1250–1382*, London (1986)

Latham, J. D., 'The Meaning of "Maydan As-Sibaq"', *Journal of Semitic Studies*, 13 (1968) pp.241–248

Latham, J. D., 'Notes on Mamlūk Horse-Archers', *Bulletin of the School of Oriental and African Studies*, 32 (1969) pp.257–267

Latham, J. D. & Paterson, W. F., *Saracen Archery*, London (1970)

Leaf, W., & Purcell, S., *Heraldic Symbols: Islamic Insignia and Western Heraldry*, London (1986)

Lézine, A., 'Les salles nobles des palais mamelouks', *Annales Islamologiques*, 10 (1972) pp.63–148 + 33 plates

Martel-Thoumian, B., 'Les Dernières Battailes du Grand Emir Yašbak Min Mahdī', in Lev, Y. (ed.), *War and Society in the Eastern Mediterranean, 7th–15th centuries*, Leiden (1996) pp.301–341

Mayer, L. A., *Mamluk Costume*, Geneva (1956)

Meinecke, M., 'Zur mamlukischen Heraldik', *Mitteilungen des Deutschen Archäologischen Instituts Abteilung Kairo*, 28 (1973) pp.213–287

Michaudel, B., 'The Use of Fortification as a Political Instrument by the Ayyubids and Mamluks in Bilād al-Shām and in Egypt (Twelfth–Thirteenth Centuries)', *Mamluk Studies Review*, 11 (2007) pp.56–67

Morillo, S., 'Mercenaries, Mamluks and Militia: Towards a Cross-cultural Typology of Military Service', in France, J. (ed.), *Mercenaries and Paid Men: The Mercenary Identity in the Middle Ages*, Leiden (2008) pp.243–260

Mufazzal Ibn Abi'l-Fazail (ed. & tr. Blochet, E.), *Histoire des Sultans Mamluks*, Paris (1919–28)

Nicolle, D., *Late Mamlūk Military Equipment* (Collection Travaux et Études de la Mission Archéologique Syro-Française, Citadelle de Damas (1999–2006): Volume III), Damascus (2011)

Nicolle, D., 'The Reality of Mamluk Warfare: Weapons, Armour and Tactics', *Al-Masāq*, 7 (1994) pp.77–100.

Öztopçu, K. (tr.), *Munyatu'l-ghuzat, A 14th Century Mamluk-Kiptchak Military Treatise* (Sources of Oriental Languages and Literatures 13), Cambridge, Mass. (1989)

Petry, C. F., 'Conjugal Rights versus Class Prerogatives: A Divorce Case in Mamlūk Cairo', in Hambly, G. R. G. (ed.), *Women in the Medieval Islamic World: Power, Patronage and Piety*, London (1998) pp.227–240

Rabbat, N. O., *The Citadel of Cairo: A New Interpretation of Royal Mamluk Architecture*, Leiden (1995)

Rabbat, N., 'The Militarization of Taste in Medieval Bilād al-Shām', in Kennedy, H. (ed.), *Muslim Military Architecture in Greater Syria*, Leiden (2006) pp.84–105

Rabie, H., *The Financial System of Egypt A.H. 564–741/A.D. 1169–1341*, Oxford (1972)

Rabie, H., 'Mamlūk Campaigns against Rhodes (A.D. 1440–1444)', in Bosworth, C. E. (ed.), *The Islamic World from Classical to Modern Times: Essays in Honour of Bernard Lewis*, Princeton (1989) pp.281–286

Röhricht, R., 'Les Batailles de Hims (1291 et 1299)', *Archives de l'Orient Latin*, 1 (1881; reprint 1964) pp.633–652

Röhricht, R., 'Les combats du Sultan Bibars, Contre les Chrétiens en Syria (1261–1277)', *Archives de l'Orient Latin*, 2 (1881; reprint 1964) pp.365–406

Sarraf, S. al-, 'Évolution du concept de furûsiyya et de sa litterature chez les Abbassides et les Mamlouks', in Delpont, E. (ed.), *Chevaux et cavaliers Arabes dans les arts d'Orient et d'Occident*, Paris (2002) pp.67–71

Sarraf, S. al-, 'Furūsiyya Literature of the Mamlūk Period', in Alexander, D. (ed.), *Furūsiyya. Volume 1: The Horse in the Art of the Near East*, Riyadh (1996) pp.118–135

Sarraf, S. al-, 'Mamlūk Furūsīyah Literature and Its Antecedents', *Mamluk Studies Review*, 8 (2004) pp.141–200

Sauvaget, J., *La Poste aux Chevaux dans L'Empire des Mamelouks*, Paris (1941)

Smith, J. M. Jr., '"Ayn Jālūt: Mamluk Success or Mongol Failure?' *Harvard Journal of Asiatic Studies*, 44 (1984) pp.307–345

Tantum, G., 'Muslim Warfare: A Study of a Medieval Muslim Treatise on the Art of War', in Elgood, R. (ed.), *Islamic Arms and Armour*, London (1979) pp.187–201

Thorau, P., 'The Battle of 'Ayn Jālūt: A Re-examination', in Edbury, P.W. (ed.), *Crusade and Settlement*, Cardiff (1985) pp.236–241

Thorau, P., *The Lion of Egypt: Sultan Baybars I & the Near East in the Thirteenth Century*, London (1987)

Van Raemdonck, M., 'Un casque mamelouk aux Musées royaux d'Art et d'Histoire á Bruxelles', in Vermeulen, U. & Smet, D. De (eds.), *Egypt and Syria in the Fatimid, Ayyubid and Mamluk Eras, II*, Leuven (1995) pp.283–294

Van Steenbergen, J., 'The Amir Yalbughā al-Khāssakī, the Qalāwūnid Sultanate, and the Cultural Matrix of Mamlūk Society: A Reassessment of Mamlūk Politics in the 1360s', *Journal of the American Oriental Society*, 131 (2011) pp.423–443

Van Steenbergen, J., 'The Mamluk Sultanate as a Military Patronage State: Household Politics and the Case of the Qalāwūnid *bayt* (1279–1382)', *Journal of the Economic and Social History of the Orient*, 56 (2013) pp.189–217

Van Steenbergen, J., 'On the Brink of a New Era? Yalbughā al-Khāssakī (d.1366) and the Yalbughāwiyah', *Mamluk Studies Review*, 15 (2011) pp.117–152

Van Steenbergen, J., 'Qalāwūnid Discourse, Elite Communication and the Mamluk Cultural Matrix: Interpreting a 14th Century Panegyric', *Journal of Arabic Literature*, 43 (2012) pp.1–28

Van Steenbergen, J., 'Ritual, Politics and the City in Medieval Cairo: The Bayn al-Qasrayn as a Mamluk "lieu de memoire", 1250–1382', in Beihammer, A. et al. (eds), *Court Ceremonies and Rituals of Power in Byzantium and the Medieval Mediterranean: Comparative Aspects*, Leiden (2013) pp.227–276.

Waterson, J., *The Knights of Islam: The Wars of the Mamluks*, London (2007)

Wiet, G., 'Les relations égypto-abyssines sous les sultans Mamlouks', *Bulletin de la Société d'archeologie copte*, 4 (1938) pp.115–140

Ziada, M. M., 'The Fall of the Mamluks 1516–1517', *Bulletin, Faculty of Arts, Foad University*, 6 (1941) pp.19–26

Ziada, M. M., 'The Mamluk Conquest of Cyprus in the Fifteenth Century', *Bulletin of the Faculty of Arts, Cairo University*, 1 (1933) pp.90–113, & 2 (1934) pp.37–57

Zoppoth, G., 'Muhammad Ibn Mängli: Ein ägyptischer Offizier und Schiftsteller des 14. Jh.s.', *Wiener Zeitschrift für die Kunde des Morgenlandes*, 53 (1957) pp.288–299

GLOSSARY

ahur	officer (*amir*) in charge of the sultan's stables
'alim	'expert'
'aliq	ration of horse fodder
amir	officer
amir al-hajj	*amir* commanding the military escort for a pilgrimage caravan to Mecca
atabak	guardian of a young prince
atabak al-'asakir	commander-in-chief of armies, second in rank to the sultan
awjaqi	young *mamluk*, not yet freed, under the authority of a training officer
bahriyah	regiment of *mamluks* established by al-Salih Ayyub
barid	postal system
bay'a	oath of allegiance
bazdar	*amir* in command of the sultan's hawking glove, with rank of *amir* of ten
dawadar	officer supervising matters relating to correspondence, the *barid* and possibly espionage
diwan	council or government department
halqa	non-*mamluk* regular troops
himaya	protection accorded to an individual or territory
imra	rank held by an *amir*
'iqta	allocation of revenues for the maintenance of an *amir*'s household and military unit
istabl	stables
iwan	room or large chamber with one wall open to the courtyard
jukandar	*amir* in charge of the sultan's polo stick

khan	secure and sometimes fortified hostel for merchants and their goods
khaznadar	the sultan's treasurer
khushdash	fellow *mamluk* of the same patron (pl. *khushdashiyah*)
mahtab	Islamic school
mamluk	man 'possessed' by another, technically a slave, but could also mean a freed slave
maq'ad	loggia of a big house, open to a courtyard
maydan	open space, often used for military training or polo
muhtasib	market inspector with legal authority
na'ib	lieutenant of the sultan
nazir al-istablat	senior administrator of the stables
qa'a	large reception hall
qala'a	citadel or castle
qasid	envoy or *mamluk* secret intelligence agent
qasr	castle, villa or palace
ra'is	commander (lit. 'head')
rabi'	fields planted with fodder for cavalry horses
rikab khanah	saddle or harness store
rikabdariyya	official in charge of the sultan's arsenal of ceremonial horse harnesses
salihiyya	*mamluks* enlisted by sultan al-Salih Ayyub, their main element being the *Bahriyah* regiment
shikar	*amir* of ten in command of the sultan's hunting animals
tabaqa	barracks or military school
taqiyah	convent of a *sufi* (dervish) order
taqlid	deed of office
tawashi	eunuch (theoretically) in charge of the education of young *mamluk* recruits
tulb	cavalry squadron
ustadar	official in charge of the household of a sultan or senior *amir*
ustadh	one possessing a recognized skill, a 'master'
wafidiyah	refugees from the Mongol Il-Khanate to the Mamluk Sultanate
wali	governor of a territory or city
waqf	Islamic pious foundation
wazir	minister or a ruler
zarbiyah	raised platform
zuwar	gang of young men, 'troublemakers'

INDEX

References to images are in bold; references to plates are in **bold** with captions in brackets.

Abkhazians 16
Acre, siege of (1291) 39, 51
Africa 6
Alans 16
alcohol 27, 34
Aleppo 21, **33**
Alexandria 20, 38
Altunbugha 50
amirs **9** (8), 10, 19, 22, 23; and home **29** (28)
Anatolia 14, 15, 53
al-Andalusi, Sa'id 7
animals 25, 50
Arabia 52
archery 44, 46
architecture **53**, **56**, 57
armour **17** (16), 43, **45** (44), 56; and horses **41** (40)
army 6, 7; and rank 23, 24; and size 21–22
arsenals 38–39
al-Ashraf Khalil, Sultan 34
Asi'l-Hadath 51
'askaris 8, 25, **38**
Aswan 52
Aybak, Sultan 26
'Ayn Jalut, battle of (1260) **9** (8), 52
Ayyubid dynasty 7–8, 10, 14, 19, 21, 38

Barquq, Sultan 22, 35
barracks 15, 42
Barsbay, Sultan 53–54
battals 31
Baybars al-Bunduqdari, Sultan 19, 22, 23, 27, 39, 47, 52
Bedouin tribes 21, 47, 52
Bertrandon de la Brocquière 35, 40
Black Sea 14
burial rituals 30
Burji regiment 16
Byzantine Empire 7, 14, 18

Cairo 10, 15, 20, 21; Citadel 18, 22, 25–26, **38**, 42, **51**, 57
camels 25, 27–28, 30, 50
campaigning 50–51
casualties 51, 53, 54
Caucasus 14
Christianity 18, 27
Circassians 16, 18, 53
clothing 25, **29** (28), 34–35, 36, 57; *see also* headgear
coast, the 24, 53
Coeur, Jacques 40
Constantinople 14, 15
craftsmen 39–40
Crimea 14, 15, 16, 19
Crusaders 18, 27, 30, 38, 47, 51–52
culture 43
Cyprus 24, 38, 53–54, **55** (54)

Dahlak Island 52
Damascus 15, 19, 20, 21, 57; and armourers 39, 40; Citadel **26**
Dawit, Emperor of Ethiopia 52–53
deserters 50
Devise des Chemins Babiloine 22
discipline 30–31, 42
drugs 34

education 43
Egypt 4, 6, 7, 14, 19, 50, 57; *see also* Cairo
Ethiopia 50, 52–53
eunuchs 19, 42

families 20–21
Fatimid Caliphate 7, 8, 19

food 14, 25, 50
furusiyah 43–44, 46, 47–48, **51**

gangs 32
garrisons 23–24
Genoa 14, 15, 16, 53
Ghassanids 18
al-Ghawri, Sultan 26
Golden Horde 14, 15

hair 34
Hajj 27
headgear 34, 35–36, 54
helmets **17** (16), **45** (44)
heraldic motifs 10, 19, 32, 36, 38
home life 32
horses 25–26, **37** (36), **41** (40), 44, **46**
Hospitallers 32, 53–54
hunting 25, 43, 46

Ibn Akhi Hizam 43
Ibn Battuta 32
Ibn Daniyal 34
Ibn Khaldun 6, 42, 50
Ibn Mangli, Muhammad 19, 44
Ibn Maymun 46
Ibn al-Mukarram 22, 24
Il-Khanate 14–15, 22, 27, 52
India 4, 6, 36
'iqta system 24
Iran 6, 7, 13, 14, 36
Islam 18, 26–28, 42
Istanbul 56

Jaqmaq, Sultan 54

khassakiyah 22–23, 25, 32
Khirokitia, battle of (1426) **55** (54)
khushdash 31–32
al-Khwarazmi 7
Kiev 14
Kipchaq 7, 14, 19, 26

Lajin, Sultan 25
language 33
Lebanon 51, 57
legal rights 5
Libya 52
lion motif **5**, **27**
literature 33–34, **53**, **57**
loyalty 5, 6, 7, 21, 42

al-Malik al-Salih, Sultan 16
Mansura, battle of (1250) 51
Marj al-Suffar, battle of (1302) 53
marriage 32–33
martyrdom 28, 30, 33
Masyaf 39
maydans 26, 47
Mecca 20, 27
Medina 20, 42
Mehmet the Conqueror 15
money 16, 24–25
Mongols 7, **9** (8), 13, 14, 19, 27, 52
al-Mu'ayyad, Sultan 22
Munyatu'l-Guzat 46
muqtas 24
museums 56
mustakhdamun 23
al-Muzaffar Hajji, Sultan 34

na'ibs 21
al-Nasir, Sultan 26, 35
naval warfare 43, 53, 54
Negus Yeshaq I, Emperor of Ethiopia 50
Nihayat al-Su'l 43–44, 46–47, 48, 50
Nubia 52
al-Nuwairi 38–39

Oghuz 7
Ottoman Empire 15, 19, 38, 54, 56

Palestine 50, 51, 57
Piloti, Emmanuel 18, 50
plague 30
Portugal 19, 27
prisoners of war 18, 51–52
Prophet Muhammad 28, 56
punishment 30–31

Qal'at al-Rum 35
Qalawun, Sultan 16, 22, 23, 25
al-Qalqashandi 22
qarani 23
Qayit Bay, Sultan 20
Qijmas al-Ishaqi 20

al-Rahba 39
Raydaniya 54
recruitment 13–16, 18–20, 42
regulations 22
relics 28, 56
Rhodes 32, 53–54
Russia 16, 18, 19

Saladin 7, 8, 36
al-Salih Ayyub, Sultan 10
sayfiya 31
scent 33
Selim the Grim, Sultan 54, 56
shamanism 26
Sidon, raids on (1382) 53
Sinai Desert 50
slavery 4–6, 7, 10; and recruitment 13–16, 21
soldiers' market 24
spirits 30
Suakin Island 52
sufis 28, 53
sultans 23
Sunni Islam 26–28
supply trains 50
Syria 4, 7, 14, 18, 50, 51, 57

al-Tabingha 50
tactics 47–48, 52
tadhkira 22
tarkhans 31
textiles 36, 38
theatre 34
Timur-i Lang 39–40, 53
trade routes 7, 14
training 40, 42, 43–44, 46–47; cavalry **49** (48)
Turkoman tribes 21, 47, 53
Turks 4, 7, 10, 14, 18, 53

Venice 14, 15
Volga Khanate 13
von Harff, Arnold 19, 42

waqf endowments 20, 51
weaponry 43, **45** (44), 56; arrows **28**, 32, 39; cannons 54; composite bows 6, 8, 14, 20; crossbows 24, 28, 34; daggers **17** (16); lasso 46; pellets 48; spears 38, 44; swords **17** (16), 22, 46–47
women 5, 32
workshops 39

al-Zahir Barquq, Sultan 35
al-Zahir Jaqmaq, Sultan 20
al-Zahir Khushqadam, Sultan 20
al-Zahir Yalbay 20
al-Zahiri 42
zuwars 19